The Man Wants His Boat

Stories of Barrow Shipyard
by Alan Lockett

Published by ALAN LOCKETT
18 Island Road
Barrow-in-Furness
Cumbria

Printed in Great Britain by
TRINITY PRESS
Farm Street
Barrow-in-Furness
Cumbria

The Man Wants His Boat

— DEDICATION —

To the shipbuilders of Barrow-in-Furness, past, present and hopefully
future

And as always my wife Audrey

— ACKNOWLEDGEMENTS —

To shipwright and tug master Dennis Quayle whose memory is far better than mine; Charlie
Allen, Peter Crosthwaite, Cameron Douglas, Derek Grundill, Tony Coulter, Bob Jones, Lol
Slee, Dennis Cullen, and other members of the Furness Retired Boilermakers and Pensioners
Association; Councillor Mrs Flo Proudfoot; All the staff of Barrow Library and Linda from
Barrow Island Branch Library; Mrs Susan Schollar for her recollection of the Pisces salvage
and the loan of Roger Chapman's book; the editor of the *North-West Evening Mail* for
permission to use articles which first appeared under the heading *Shipyard Life* and *Lockett's
Locker* and for the use of photographs; VSEL for permission to use photographs from their
collection; P&O Group for permission to use photographs from their collection; Bryn
Trescatheric for permission to climb on his shoulders; No 31 District Committee of the
Confederation of Shipbuilding and Engineering Unions for their kind permission to use
extracts from *The Strike*; Mike Gardner for his encouragement in the writing of this book;
Alen McFadzean who had been there and knew what it was about but still had the difficult
task of putting my writings in order; Anne McFadzean for her typing; the staff of the Dock
Museum; Allan Smith for his excellent photographic work; Heather Horner at the *Evening
Mail* library; and special thanks to Jim Glasgow for his flattering foreword.

This book has been grant aided by the Kirby Archives Trust, administered by Cumbria County
Council's Archive Service.

— CONTENTS —

— FOREWORD —

THIS book by Alan Lockett, *The Man Wants His Boat,* tells a story of people who were involved in building ships at Barrow-in-Furness in the shipyard where Alan and I spent our working lives.

Alan Lockett and I were fellow pupils at Barrow Grammar School in the wartime years. Not for him the routine of the newly-formed school cadet unit, Alan joined the local Sea Cadets, the start of an association that lasted for many years.

After leaving school Alan became an apprentice shipwright with Vickers Armstrong Ltd and throughout his career was able to pursue his passionate interest in all aspects of ships, shipbuilding, boats and boating.

For many years Alan Lockett's name appeared above a weekly column in the *Barrow News* and later the *Evening Mail.* The content and style earned praise from many quarters, the column was widely read and interest extended beyond the boating fraternity.

This story has been written, warts and all, by a man who worked at the sharp end of shipbuilding. Many people, not just shipbuilders, will be fascinated by the detail of working life conveyed in these pages.

In shipbuilding and naval parlance, the term boat is used for a submarine. This did not inhibit one foreman in the use of "The Man wants his Boat" as a routine exhortation. Many expressions used were far less polite! The author's perception reveals many characters with their own idiosyncratic expressions, habits, methods and mannerisms.

A well-deserved tribute is paid to the skills of shipwrights and loftsmen. I can personally vouch for many of those named by the author. Each shipyard trade had its own craft skills and within each department there were men who earned the respect of their colleagues by virtue of exceptional ability and they were recognised by their peers across trade boundaries.

There is mention of industrial conflict and, from time to time, this unfortunately became part of the scene. However, the one message that shipyard people did recognise was "The Man wants his Boat", and this was never more in evidence than at launch and sea trials. The team-work involved was without parallel but sadly this could not be maintained on a day-to-day basis.

Alan is correct in his reference to the huge amount of ballast fitted in the

Chusan. At a late stage of construction the Peninsular and Oriental Steam Navigation Company decided that Chusan should have a cruising role and, with no cargo to be carried in the forward holds, it was decided to fit permanent ballast to maintain trim and stability. If this changed role had been specified at the design stage the Vickers naval architects would have had a more elegant solution but there was no error on their part.

The captain of Chusan had a horseshoe mounted on one of the forward poppets at launch, it was later mounted in his cabin. Alan does not say whether the shipwrights mounted the horseshoe upside down although this possibility was dismissed as a cause of the fore-poppet collapse!

At Barrow shipyard no two customers were the same and no two contracts were the same. There were tough times but the overriding recollection is one of considerable achievement. Success of any business venture depends on people and Alan Lockett's story is about the people whose companionship Alan and I shared during our industrial careers.

Alan and I were both involved with the Furness Maritime Trust, whose principal objective is the formation of a maritime museum in Furness. This book well illustrates Alan's commitment to maritime history.

Alan Lockett is a well-deserved holder of the British Empire Medal, awarded for services to shipbuilding, maritime history and charity. In recent years a number of local authors have put pen to paper on topics of local interest and *The Man Wants His Boat,* one man's view of the history of Barrow shipyard over almost fifty years, is a worthy and welcome additional volume.

Jim Glasgow
former Deputy Managing Director
VSEL
Barrow-in-Furness

— INTRODUCTION —

SHIPYARD histories are, in the main, written by historians, directors, naval architects and the like who tell of how a shipyard operates, but nothing of the rank and file workmen — who do the work — and of how they earn their wages.

This book, based on my own experiences as a time-served tradesman working for more than 44 years in the Barrow shipyard, is written, hopefully, to tell something about the conditions which prevailed and the craftsmen and characters who worked alongside me.

In some cases the names have been changed for obvious reasons. The dates quoted are from the *North-West Evening Mail* although some are from memory. Opinions expressed are my own unless otherwise stated.

Of the ships, more than eleven hundred of them, ranging from a five-ton yacht, built in 1886 at a cost of 210 to the 16,000 tonne, 500 million Trident submarines of today, they have been well documented and recorded in other books although some of their stories have yet to be told.

When during the early 1950s I was serving on Barrow-built passenger liners as an assistant carpenter, I was often asked where my home town was. The conversation then generally took the form of a geography lesson, where I informed the inquirer that Barrow was not situated on the Clyde, Tyne or Mersey, and was, in fact, a shipbuilding town in its own right and the birthplace of many fine ships.

To set the scene for this book, the location of the town and its shipyard are essential if the reader is to appreciate the stories of the shipbuilders of Barrow.

Although the accent is mainly on the shipbuilding side of the yard, I am sure that many employed in the engineering side will be able to relate to and recall some of the people and the events which occurred during the past fifty years.

The title *The Man wants his Boat* is from an old shipyard saying, often used by the foremen, to their men, to signify that brew, or break time, was over and they should be moving back to their work.

Chapter 1

The Barrow Shipyard — a Brief History

THE fortunes and growth of Barrow-in-Furness, a town on the north-west coast of England, were founded on the rich hæmatite iron ore deposits of the area which led to the establishment of iron and steel works.

Their expansion, aided by the Furness Railway Company which built the giant Barrow docks, seemed a logical move towards the setting up of a shipyard.

Sir James Ramsden, general manager of the railway, was the prime mover in the promotion of the Barrow Shipbuilding Company. On 28 January 1871 at Ramsden's home at Abbotswood, near Furness Abbey, Ramsden and the local business men and entrepreneurs formed the Barrow Shipbuilding Company and on 18 February 1871 the new company was registered with an authorised capital of £100,000 in 4,000 shares of £25.

At the same time an independent company was formed to trade with Barrow, India and China by way of the canal. Known as the Eastern Steamship Company, it had a total authorised capital of £500,000 in 500 shares of £1,000 each.

The two ventures, shipbuilding and ship-owning, were closely connected and in March 1871 it was agreed that the Barrow Shipbuilding Company should build four steamers for the Eastern Steamship Company at a cost of £60,000.

And so, shipbuilding came to Barrow.

The above brief details about the formation of Barrow's major shipyard — there were other small wooden shipbuilders in the area before this — were taken from Tom Clark's book, *A Century of Shipbuilding,* published in 1971.

The shipyard has traded under various names since its formation. In 1888 it was the Naval Construction and Armaments Company which later became Vickers Sons and Maxim Limited. In 1911 the title was Vickers Limited. Still later, in the mid 1920s, the amalgamation of Vickers and Armstrong Whitworth led to the title of Vickers Armstrong Limited. Other titles were Vickers Limited Shipbuilding Group, Vickers Shipbuilding Group Limited — a subsidiary of British Shipbuilders — and later, upon privatisation,

Vickers Shipbuilding and Engineering Limited Consortium plc, or VSEL Consortium plc. A later name change agreed at the eighth annual general meeting in July 1993 led to the shorter Vickers Shipbuilding and Engineering Limited. But as the poet said: "What's in a name?" To the people of Barrow, who have either known of or worked in the shipyard over the years, and whose social and economic life has been dependent on the fortunes of the shipyard as it became the town's main industry, the name is immaterial. Two words sum it up. The Yard.

At its peak in January 1917 the shipyard employed 31,000 people. During the depression years of the 1920s and 30s the total workforce was down to 3,150.

The stories and recollections in this book cover the period from 1944 to 1991 and despite the many changes of name, I am sure that the word shipyard or yard will suffice to identify the place where I and thousands like me earned a living.

Chapter 2

A Job in the Yard — Apprenticeship

BEFORE World War Two most boys left school at fourteen, worked in the yard as an office boy then began a five-year apprenticeship at their chosen trade at about sixteen.

This system still applied when I left Barrow Grammar School in February 1944 and visited Vickers Labour Bureau, as it then was, at the office alongside Kings Gate.

Getting my first job presented no problem. Five minutes after asking if there were any vacancies for an office boy I was on my way home again with instructions to report for work at 7:30am the following day.

I was a month short of my fifteenth birthday when I started as an office boy to Raymond Sankey, head of Vickers Civil Defence. My job was to issue steel helmets and equipment to workmen as they reported for firewatching.

Every workman over the age of seventeen who was not in the Home Guard, Auxiliary Fire Service or Civil Defence had to spend, I think, one night a month in the yard, firewatching. This involved spending a full night on top of a crane or on the roof of a high building ready to report the location of fires which could have been caused by German bombs during an air raid. There is a memorial plaque on the 150-ton crane at Buccleuch Dock which commemorates the death of two men who were firewatching on the previous crane on that site. On the night of 7-8 May 1941 it was brought down by enemy action. One of the men was an apprentice fitter aged only seventeen.

However, back to my first job.

Another chore was to carry messages around the yard to the four civil defence stations manned 24 hours a day. My immediate superior was a retired policeman whose main occupation appeared to be slurping tea from a mug the size of a small bucket.

Within days of starting the job, for which I was paid 14s 6d (72p) for a 47-hour week, I became aware that life among the men was far removed from that of a schoolboy.

My superior was like many other persons who, given a little authority, adopt a supercilious attitude. This always came to the fore when he stood at the counter dealing with the workmen. On one occasion his attitude as he

13

placed his "bucket" on the counter was somewhat overbearing and the workman in question did not appear too happy. After a minute or two the workman interrupted and said: "Excuse me, but were you once a policeman?" Told "Yes" he said: "Did you have a beat on Walney Island?" Again the reply was "Yes". At this the workman reached across the counter, grabbed my boss by his coat lapels, punched him on the nose then poured the bucket of tea over his head. "I've been waiting many years to meet up with you again and to get even for what you did", he said. As my boss sat on the floor with a glazed look on his face, tea leaves in his hair and the blood streaming from his nose and mixing with the tea running down his shirt, the workman calmly signed for his equipment, wished me good morning and left.

As a member of the Sea Cadets and keen on boats and boating it seemed that the best apprenticeship for me was that of a shipwright, so after six months as an office boy I presented myself to the head foreman shipwright to ask about serving my time. Waiting outside his office at the top yard I stood for about ten minutes gazing up at the aircraft carrier under construction in Number 1 Berth. This was HMS Majestic, later to become HMAS Melbourne.

Tommy Dennis, or TD as he was known to his tradesmen, was a head foreman of the old school. When I was at last called in to see him, by his clerk George, he was sat in his wooden office glaring like a starved vulture. His symbol of office, a shiny bowler hat, was on his desk and his shiny, crumpled navy-blue suit almost reflected the light from the unshaded light bulb which barely illuminated the wooden hut with its paint peeling from the walls. Mr Dennis — no one, not even his most trusted foreman, ever addressed him by his first name — peered over his spectacles which hung precariously from the end of his hooked nose and said: "Why do want to be a shipwright sonny?" I could only stammer out such statements as: " . . . always wanted to work on ships, all my friends are apprentice shipwrights and I thought it would be a good trade to follow . . ." He replied: "You look as though you'll grow big enough for the work. Get a note from George the clerk, take it to the clinic for a medical examination and start work Monday morning."

So it was as simple as that.

As I walked back to my office boy work, through the pouring rain, I wondered just what I had let myself in for and, most of all, would I be able to climb up to and work on the high stagings which surrounded the many ships being built at the top yard?

Looking back at the ease with which I obtained my first job, then later my apprenticeship, I can only sympathise with the young men of today who have to undergo the trauma of obtaining good exam results, filling in countless application forms, talking with career advisors, enduring interviews and job aptitude tests then suffering the agonies of waiting months to find out whether they have been successful in gaining job.

Life was obviously more simple then than it is today. Having passed a rudimentary medical examination at the shipyard clinic I reported for work as an apprentice shipwright at the age of fifteen-and-a-half.

The system of being given indentures, whereby a deposit of £5 was required and the firm guaranteed you employment for five years while teaching you a trade, was not in being during the war years. In fact, I think it was not re-established after the war although agreements were signed by parents and certificates of apprenticeship given upon completion of the required period. As far as I can recall there were no forms to sign either by my parents or myself, and no written conditions of employment were ever produced.

My wage was 17s 6d (87p) for a 47-hour, five-and-a-half-day week and like most other apprentices when first commencing their trade, I started work in the shipwrights workshop or, more aptly and traditionally named, the spar shed. This was a long building situated near the Devonshire Gate, or South Gate as it is called today. At the time, September 1944, it was quite a busy place with about twenty shipwrights employed.

The first tradesman I worked with — strange how one can recall such details — was George Carter, a character of uncertain age, reputed to be well over seventy, whose job it was to make temporary wooden ladders for use on the ships under construction. I can't remember much about my actual part in making these ladders but I did learn many other things which stood me in good stead throughout the years.

There were about thirty apprentice shipwrights scattered throughout the yard and with three other lads, who were new starters the same as me, we longed to be out on the ships. The experienced shipwrights in the spar shed were always willing to teach us the skills of the trade as it was then. The shipwrights trade was in those days, very much like the ships, nothing if not traditional and work practices were much as they had been for many years.

Masts and spars were made by the shipwrights. The warships tubular steel masts were usually assembled by George Dickinson and Freddie Watts. The wooden spars, boat booms and masts, also made by the same men in the long narrow part of the spar shed, were to me and my fellow apprentices real works of art and fine examples of the shipwrights' trade. Traditional ship-wrights' tools, the broad axe, adze, draw knife and jack plane wielded by these men could transform a 25ft log of Oregon or Colombian pine into a spar or mast with a finish like glass.

I recall that a few years later the same men produced and erected, at Craven Park, a new goal post for Barrow Rugby Club. The job was accomplished within a couple of days after the original posts had been blown down in a gale. This would have been around 1947-48 in the days when Barrow RL could, and did, beat their arch rivals Wigan on many occasions. No matter that the new post stood about ten feet higher than its mate at the other end of the crossbar, it never appeared to detract from the goal kicking of Joe Jones or Willie Horne. The goal post was taken to Craven Park for erection by the reliable transport allocated to the shipwrights department — one horse and a flat cart!

It seems strange to look back and think that when Britain was fighting a war and ships and armaments were desperately needed, the transport of equipment and material around the yard was dependent upon the speed of a horse.

This transport was hired in from an outside contractor and the horse, a large white one whose name I can't recall, was to us young apprentices as grumpy and bad tempered as its unsociable old driver. Even if offered one of our sandwiches, the horse would also attempt to take off our hands. With boys being boys, as the saying goes, it was not unusual for the lads to put wedges behind the brakes and under the wheels of the cart in addition to tying a rope from the cart to the adjacent timber racks. This practice was not to the liking of the driver or the horse and the driver, whose name I think was Steve, would threaten us with all kinds of punishments if he ever caught us.

But the shipwrights in the spar shed tolerated us and any intelligent questions about the trade always received an answer and very often a demonstration of how to do a certain job.

The foreman shipwright over the spar shed was Tommy Dickinson, a local Tory councillor who was noted for his easy-going ways. If he saw the head foreman heading towards the workshop he would rush out of his office to warn everyone to look busy. He too tolerated the apprentices. Often, on cold winter mornings, we would go into the spar shed to meet our mates and to get warm before going aboard the ships we were working on. To chase the lads to their work, Tommy Dickinson would come out of his office and shout, "Come on me hearties, square your yards. The man wants his boat." This exhortation usually got the lads moving, albeit reluctantly.

The same character was also fond of telling us not to sit on the hot water pipes because "when you get older you'll get piles." He was right. Some of us did. I recall his retirement day. At the age of 65 Tommy Dickinson lifted a 56lb weight in each hand and raised them above his head several times just to show how fit he was.

It was while working in the spar shed that I and the other lads got our tools. With the help of shipwrights like Hughie Costley and Davy (Skipper) Reid, a list of shipwright's tools was compiled for approval by head foreman

16

Tommy Dennis. Once he agreed to the list and signed it, tools could be obtained from the general store and a tool box obtained from the joiners shop.

The tool boxes which were made by apprentice joiners were peculiar to the shipwrights trade, being more of a tool chest with a top opening lid. For some reason that I have never been able to discover, this type of box was always known as a donkey. The smaller tool boxes issued later were of a standard issued to the apprentice joiners and were of a smaller upright type. These too had a name — Yankee. There was a suggestion from the old shipwrights that these smaller boxes were more suitable for seagoing carpenters who served on American or Yankee ships. Apparently, the conditions would be so bad on an American vessel that the carpenter only needed a small tool box because he wouldn't be staying that long.

The tools obtained were, to quote the old timers: "Everything a joiner would use plus the tools that a skilled craftsman, like a shipwright would need." Obviously these were saws, planes, chisels, drills etc plus the shipwright's special tools such as an adze, maul (large hammer), long drills called augers and the traditional caulking irons and mallet. These tools were definitely not a gift from the firm. They were sold to us at cost price and I think that my set of tools cost around £6. This sum was paid back to the firm at the rate of 2s (10p) a week, stopped out of my wages.

All apprentices were taught how to grind and sharpen their tools and given help by the tradesmen to fit a shaft for their adze.

The making of a box for our carborundum sharpening stones was encouraged. It had to be of teak wood for some reason, and despite the war and the fact that no timber had been imported into the country for years, there was always a good supply of wood available, even if it had to be quietly acquired from the nearby timber racks. If the lid on the box would fit either way and not fall off when turned upside down it was judged that we had made a success of the job.

How proud we were of our shiny new tools and how we longed for the day when we would be using them out on the ships, laying and caulking decks, fitting handrail and doing all the other woodworking jobs associated with our trade.

It was during these early days of my apprenticeship that I became aware that not all the shipwright tradesmen were paid the same rate. Some in the spar shed, by virtue of their work for different ships under construction, were booked to the ship's contract and paid at a higher rate, just over £5 a week I think it was. Other men were on time-rate. This was like maintenance work and the rate was about £1 a week less than the contract rate.

Some young tradesmen working in the spar shed were classed as safetymen. Their job was to make temporary wooden gratings for the ships under construction and to fit them, and temporary ladders and safety rails. They were classed as time-workers and received the lower rate.

Some older shipwrights would leave the workshop each morning loaded up like Snow White's seven dwarfs, with picks and shovels and double-handed crosscut saws. These men were also on the time rate and their job was to work on the maintenance of the shipbuilding berths. The building berths at this time were not concreted and this squad had to dig down through the earth to repair and replace the groundlogs and wooden slipway foundations.

This anomaly of different rates for different jobs was a source of contention, particularly among the younger men.

After about six weeks in the spar shed I had my tools, knew some of the men and a very small amount about the shipwrights' trade. I did, however, know how to identify different types of timber. This knowledge was essential for apprentices who had to be sure that they obtained the correct kind of firewood for their mates.

Another very important piece of knowledge for the young apprentice was the art of brewing tea and this, as will be told in a later chapter, could be fraught with many hazards and problems.

Eventually the call came. Tommy Dickinson called me to one side and said: "Report to Mr McGruer in the morning for outfit work on the aircraft carrier."

Chapter 3

A Shipyard Comes to Life

SHIPBUILDING practices in 1944 and the way of life on the shipbuilding berths were much the same as when the yard opened in the 1870s.

As I stood outside the top yard time office awaiting the arrival of foreman shipwright George McGruer on a grey autumn morning with the outlines of the tower cranes strengthening as the daylight increased with the clearing away of the morning mist, I was able to witness a shipyard coming to life.

Certain workmen arrived at the yard early.

Timekeepers were usually first to commence work and their wooden huts with a window on each of its six sides were always open for business at 7am. The method of timekeeping in those days could not have been simpler. Every workman had a number and this number was engraved on two brass discs about the size of a 50p piece. These discs, called checks, were kept in a similarly numbered slot on a large wooden tray. When the workman came to check on, he would shout his number to the timekeeper, or office boy or girl, at the appropriate window and be given one check, which he kept. This check was kept in his possession throughout the day then thrown into a box at the gate when he finished work at 5pm, or 7pm if he was working over. This check was also his identification throughout the day, the other check was put into a box in the time office to be later put back in its slot. When the 7:30am buzzer had ceased blowing, any checks still left in the tray signified that their owners were not in work.

Should the owner arrive late, before 8am, he had to report to the time office to be booked in and his wages were then calculated accordingly with the late time deducted. Four late starts a month were allowed before the workman had to report to his head foreman who could then refuse to let him work the shift.

During the war this system was relaxed somewhat owing to possible transport delays due to enemy action.

A 7am start was the norm for the drivers of steam trains and steam cranes who had to load up with their ration of coal and then stoke up the fires ready for steaming at 7:30am. Rivet heaters or hotting lads, who were always men in my days, also had to light their coke fires. It also paid them, after having drawn their coke ration, to be early at the machine store to draw out their compressed-air screwing-up machines, or impact wrenches, for their riveting squad.

These tools were usually in short supply and the shipwrights, or their apprentices, often had to fall back on Armstrong's Patent, this being shipyard jargon for brute strength. In this context it meant the use of a spanner with a 6ft length of pipe on the handle to tighten up the three-quarter or seven-eighth diameter bolts which secured the hull or deck plating to the frames or beams.

Around 7:20am the influx of workmen would increase with hundreds hurrying through the gates to lift their checks. No workmen came to work in a car. Even if they were one of the very few to own a vehicle, the rationing effectively prohibited its use.

Transport to work was usually by bicycle, always an old one as new ones were not available during the war. Those who lived on the outskirts of town would use the buses and the men from Dalton, Ulverston, Askam and Millom would arrive by train, disembarking at the long-since demolished station on Island Road.

A roar, then a constant hiss from down the berths, would indicate that the millwrights had turned on the wind, or compressed-air. The smell of wood smoke and sulphur would be borne on the breeze from the ships which signified that the rivet heaters were lighting their coal fires.

A last minute rush to the time offices by the last minute arrivals and the notes of the 7:30am buzzer died away in the early morning air. A new working day had begun in the Barrow shipyard.

In those days there were few workshops or stores for the tradesmen to keep their tools in and consequently most would go straight aboard the ships they were working on. Welders, both men and women, would collect their quivers of welding rods from the rod store. Caulkers, riveters and holder-ups would draw their windy hammers and riveting guns from the machine store, then hundreds of shipyard workers, representing dozens of trades, would begin the trek to their respective work areas. Some of the black trades such as caulkers and riveters would have to report to their foremen on the market. This was held at the top of the berths, outside the platers shed. Once there, they would be allocated specific jobs or work areas by their respective foremen.

Within minutes of the cessation of the buzzer, the tempo of activity would increase. A railway engine would chug its way down the ramp alongside the berths, pulling wagons loaded with shell plates, frames, decks, and bulk-heads, in fact, all the varied components of steelwork required to construct a ship, be it cargo vessel, aircraft carrier, destroyer or submarine.

Mobile steam cranes would ramble by, hissing, spitting, spluttering and clanking as they wheezed their way to their work areas.

The sound of steel cylinders rattling around the yard was also a familiar noise in the early morning. These were the oxygen and acetylene gas bottles used by the burners. Their labourers, somewhat aptly named bottle rollers, would throw them off the lorries then roll them down the berths ready to be slung aboard by crane. This practice discontinued in, I think, the 1960s because it was highly dangerous and the possible cause of explosions.

When Mr McGruer came out of the head foreman's office to take me aboard the aircraft carrier HMS Majestic, to introduce me to the tradesman I would be working with, his first words were: "How old are you sonny?" When I replied: "Fifteen-and-a-half," he pointed up to the staging which surrounded the hull of the three-quarters built ship and said: "When you go up there on the staging, if anyone asks your age, tell 'em you're sixteen." I learned later that under the safety laws of the day you had to be sixteen years old before going on staging more than 10ft above the ground.

As we climbed the steep gangway which terminated at hangar deck level, the ship was already buzzing with activity.

Going aboard with us were many other workmen. Practically everyone was carrying something. Plumbers were carrying tools, pipes and lengths of steel rods, used for determining the shape of pipes. Fitters had valves and tool bags and various other bits and pieces. Red leaders, about whom more later, had their paint pots and brushes. Shipwrights and their apprentices carried bags of tools, large spanners made in the blacksmiths shop, bags of bolts and washers, coils of wire and much other equipment which later I was able to identify and use. Platers, too, carried lengths of angle bar, small brackets and even lengths of thin wood, called batten, as I learned later to cut and fit to the shape of the plates they needed. In fact, everyone conveyed the impression that they knew what they were doing, where they were going, and were intent on the business of building a ship.

Once aboard and in their work areas everyone's first job was to pick up a discarded welding rod — the deck was usually littered with them — bend it into a hook and push it through a rivet hole or over a bulkhead and then hang their coat or haversack on it. Then they would start work.

Hopefully no burner or welder would start work in the area of their improvised coat hanger and send their jacket up in flames. There was no compensation if such an event occurred.

As I was guided through the maze of passageways and down vertical ladders in occasionally semi-darkness to where the outfit shipwrights had their temporary store for tools and equipment, I became aware of the noise. This usually began with a solo staccato rattle as a caulker tried out his windy hammer to blow out the oil. Then an impact wrench would join in as someone inserted and tightened extra bolts in his riveting area. The ironwork shipwrights, too, would add to the crescendo of noise as they used their impact wrenches and then their mauls to drive in steel wedges or to hammer a deck or bulkhead to the required position.

When the work aboard such a ship as an aircraft carrier was in full flight the noise was indescribable. Not just ordinary noise but an ever increasing cacophony of sound that rose up from the compressed-air hammer of the machine caulkers and riveting squads. It seemed to echo throughout the ship like the continuous roaring of a huge waterfall.

To talk normally in this bedlam of sound was virtually impossible. To counteract this the shipbuilders had, over the years, devised their own form of sign language. To ask the time you made a motion similar to that of pulling a pocket-watch from a waistcoat pocket. The reply would be given in sign language. An arm movement across the waist meant half past the hour, and if followed by three raised fingers the time was half past three. Similarly, if the arm movement was made at neck level it would mean either quarter to or quarter past the hour. This would depend on whether two fingers were raised first or a downward sweep of the hand was made, the latter signifying past the hour.

A warning of, or inquiry about, the whereabouts of the supervisors was also done in sign language. Two fingers placed across the arm between the elbow and shoulder referred to a chargehand. Three fingers referred to a foreman. Making the outline of a trilby hat on your head related to a head foreman and the impression of a bowler hat signified a manager.

Possibly finger gestures went back to the days of World War One in the trenches, two fingers for a corporal etc. The raising of seven fingers related to the seven minutes allowed for time at the toilet. A clerk in the toilet took your check or check number to ensure the time limit was not exceeded.

Signals to the crane drivers in their cabs high above the berths were done by whistle and hand movements. Three blasts to raise, two to lower and one to stop.

With the noise in the shipyard it was no wonder it was said you could always tell a boilermaker or shipbuilder by the way he shouted in someone's ear while looking around for signs of his foreman approaching.

Working hours during the war and for a couple of years after were 47 hours a week; overtime, three nights a week until 7pm and alternate Saturday afternoons or Sundays, was compulsory. If a workman refused a certain amount of overtime he was taken to a tribunal and either warned or fined. If he persisted with the offence he would be conscripted into the armed forces. All shipyard workers were classed as being in a reserved occupation and were not allowed to leave the yard or transfer to other jobs.

Everything in those days was in short supply and conditions in the yard were extremely primitive. No toilet paper was supplied, at least not for the workmen, and washing facilities were few and far between. It was not uncommon for the workmen to bring their sandwiches for lunch wrapped up in the previous day's *Daily Mirror* and then later use the same newspaper for attending to the wants of nature.

Members of the shipwrights launchway squad would come back to their store at the end of a shift covered in grease, soft soap and tallow to wash their hands in a bucket of warm water. They would use the soft soap from the launchways as a washing and cleansing agent. This was done in strict rotation, or pecking order as we would say today. The squad leader always had the first dip in the bucket followed by senior shipwrights and regular members of the squad. By the time the junior shipwrights and labourers came to wash their hands the water was like glutinous mud.

The launchway squad was one section of the shipwrights trade that, with the building of Devonshire Dock Hall and the lowering of ships into the dock, has possibly gone for ever, but mention of it brings to mind some of the characters who worked at this laborious task. All the launchway squad, both shipwrights and their labourers, were big strong men. They had to be for their work was exacting and heavy. The squad leader for many years was Bert Jeavons, who in later years was awarded the British Empire Medal for his services to shipbuilding. Another well-known character in this squad was Alan Newsham, of North Scale on Walney, commonly known as Big Hefty. Alan was a gentle giant, a one-time rugby league front row forward who played for the then Liverpool Stanley team. To say he was a big man would be something of an understatement. In fact, it could be said that the Devonshire Dock Hall was designed from his measurements.. To see Big Hefty pick up two 12in square logs of timber and carry them one under each arm down through the ankle-deep mud of the building berth, then effortlessly throw them in place on top of the slipways to form part of the launch cradle, was to see a man of action ideally suited to his work.

Most of the launchway squad wore clogs for their work under the bottom of the ships. Their skills included not only the positioning of launchways and packings but also the fitting of the heavy timbers to the exact shape of the ship's hull to form a perfect cradle to support the thousands of tons of ship on its way down the berth into its natural element.

Other launchway squad members of the time were Jack Brewer, Joe Darragh and Jack Sergeant Snr. In later years men such as Charlie Allen, Bill Milburn and John Harris carried on this work until the last conventional launch into Walney Channel of HM Submarine Talent, on Friday 15 April 1988, effectively made their skills redundant.

However, back to the wartime years.

Thermos flasks were unheard of and one duty of the apprentice was to brew up for his tradesman. The conical-shaped tin brew-can, with its lid that served as a cup, cost 1/- (5p) at the local ironmongers. Tea and sugar were carried in a double-ended oval-shaped container, tea at one end and sugar in the other. This mixture was usually sufficient for two brews if judiciously used.

Brewing up was accomplished by various methods. If you were friendly with a rivet heater or hotting lad, you could utilise his coke fire, but you had to take your turn in the queue. If you could persuade a burner, he would heat your water with his burning torch or you could boil your can on the plate bending furnaces in the platers shed. The two latter methods had their disadvantages. If the burner was not careful he could soon burn a hole in your can. If utilising the furnaces and Mr Noel Emmett, the little bandy-legged foreman plater, approached the area, a quick get-away was essential otherwise a report would be made to your head foreman. Mr Emmett did not like apprentices and a quick get-away often meant leaving your can over the furnace opening. On your return it was not uncommon to find the can glowing red hot with the bottom burnt out. This situation, needless to say, did not always go down too well with the owner of the brew can. The stories of certain managers kicking over the brew cans in front of their owners, I can confirm were certainly true.

Another chore for the apprentice was the acquisition of firewood for his mate. Many lengths of stage planking were cut up into 6in lengths to keep the home fires burning. Cobs of coal from the steam cranes and railway engines also supplemented the demand for fuel at home. It was a requisite of the tradesman that the firewood be of a certain type. If whitewood was used it was reputed to chase the cat around the kitchen due to the sparks given off. Therefore the apprentice had to be able to identify the correct types of wood which were suitable for this task. In later years the introduction of gas and electric fires, coupled with central heating in the home, eliminated the demand for shipyard firewood — or kettle wedges as it was sometimes called.

Conditions aboard a ship under construction were almost indescribable. Apart from the noise, workmen had to put up with coke fumes from the riveters' fires and fumes from the welders. Extraction fans were unknown. And then there was the never ending rust.

Ship's plates were only painted during the latter stages of construction and if they had lain on the berths for any length of time they soon developed a coating of rust. One blow from the shipwright's maul or the plater's plying hammer and everyone in the vicinity would get a cascade of rust down their neck. To counter this, all shipyard workers wore flat caps which doubled as gloves when holding fittings for the welder to tack-weld in position. Red leaders, the semi-skilled painters of the day, were in abundance and they too added to the noise as they chipped and scaled the rust from the ship's plating.

These men were on piecework and on HMS Majestic their work had to be passed by a naval overseer before payment could be approved.

One such overseer, named Mr Hutton, was unpopular with these hard-working red leaders because he often condemned their work and made them do the whole lot again without extra payment. Mr Hutton was a pompous, self-important character, small of stature but with a big opinion of himself — and he always wore a blue suit instead of the customary distinctive overseer's brown overalls. His habit of sneaking around the ship peering through doorways at the red leaders certainly incensed the men. But one day they got their revenge.

I recall working on the shell side of the aircraft carrier when Mr Hutton came along the staging, peering through the portholes and obviously spying on the red leaders in an attempt to catch them applying paint without adequate plate preparation. As he stood by one porthole in his smart blue suit, a hand bearing a large paint brush leaded with red lead paint shot out. Before he could move the brush plastered him from neck to waist then moved on to a horizontal stroke across his chest, effectively covering him with paint. As he stood there gasping with shock and amazement the hand and brush were swiftly withdrawn and the porthole clanged shut from the inside. As uninvolved observers of this incident, my mate and I burst out laughing as the little overseer climbed down from the staging with the sign of the cross, in red lead, dripping from his clothes. Following this incident Mr Hutton wore overalls, but I am unaware if his attitude towards the red leaders improved any.

As the ships in those days were built on the berth plate by plate, similar to the construction of a Meccano model, probably the most dangerous job of all was that of the shipwright steel erectors, or hanging-up squads as they were known.

Two shipwrights, a labourer and an apprentice usually constituted a squad and their work was hard, heavy and skilful. It entailed unloading steel frames, bulkheads and beams, as they were brought down by railway wagons from the platers shed at the top of the berths. All the platework structures were identified with location numbers and they had to be sorted out before being slung, by crane, to the required position on the ship then erected and secured.

Jack Marsh, or Mazzie, came from Ulverston and was arguably the hardest working hanger-up squad leader in the shipyard. Thick set, always with tidy, blue overalls and a ruddy complexion under his flat cap, he could climb up a swaying and unsupported ship's frame hand over hand, using staging bolts in the rivet holes for hand and foot-grips to let go the shackle from the crane wire. He could walk confidently along a 3in-wide beam high above the decks with a drop of 50ft below him to unfasten the eyebolt from the crane. In short he — like his fellow hanger-up shipwrights Snowy Hill, Bill Watts, Jack Rorison, Fred Bushell and Jimmy Costley — had the agility of a monkey, the strength of Geoff Capes and the skill and expertise that could position and secure a 50-ton section of ship within an eighth of an inch from its final position.

Men like these worked in all weathers, freezing cold when their spanners, pinch bars and shackles had to be warmed over a fire to prevent breakage by the frost. In the pouring rain they had only their own coats or an ex-Home Guard greatcoat to protect them from the elements. In the hottest weather, in their shirtsleeves, they would erect the ship plate by plate until it stood ready for launch. Yet for all their hazardous work, none of which they would be allowed to practise today thanks to the Health and Safety at Work Act, I can recall few instances of the hanger-ups suffering any serious injuries or being involved in any accidents.

It was during these first few months of my apprenticeship that I began to realise that the shipwright's trade had many variations of jobs and skills. Over the next forty or so years I was to work at most of these jobs and meet a host of interesting characters.

Shipbuilders then, as now, were composed of two types of craftsmen. The black trades were platers, shipwrights, blacksmiths, riveters and welders — in the main the men who constructed the ship's hull. The outfit trades were joiners, painters, electricians, plumbers, sheet metal workers and engineers whose task was to fit out and finish the ship.

To complicate the system somewhat, shipwrights, and also some sections of the engineering trades, were involved in both the building and outfitting of the ship.

Most trades had a hard core of men for each specialised type of work, who moved from ship to ship doing the same class of work on each.

In the outfit squad of shipwrights with whom I worked on HMS Majestic were men who had moved on to the vessel after completing similar work on the aircraft repair ship HMS Pioneer. Johnny McAteer, the squad leader whose brothers Dave and Paddy were also shipwrights, worked on the installation and fitting out of the aircraft lifts and deck arrester gear. Bill Brooks always worked on the fitting of ladders, stanchions and guard rails. Liner-off Arthur Hepworth was the man who could fit far more ammunition in the magazine of a warship than the plans catered for, and this skill was appreciated by each ship's gunnery officer who always adopted his suggestions.

Chapter 4

Characters and Conditions

AT THE beginning of 1945 I was transferred, along with my mate shipwright Clem Dennis, brother of head foreman Tommy Dennis, to work in the shipwrights repair squad. Based at Buccleuch Dock this squad had, under the leadership of foreman Harry Waterhouse, done sterling work throughout the war. They fendered in, docked and repaired, on both the floating dock and graving dock, damaged warships such as the British destroyer HMS Eskimo and the Canadian destroyer HMCS Saguenay, both of which had arrived in Barrow minus their bows. They had worked all hours in all conditions, repairing and refitting the merchant ships that had entered the port, damaged either by enemy action or stress of weather.

The repair manager was Mr Bernard (Barney) Oughtred who walked with a limp reputed to have been sustained while playing international rugby union before the war. The repair squad had a variety of jobs. One day they could be repairing the timber belting on the dock wall, the next they could be working on a merchant ship at Ramsden Dock or preparing the floating or graving docks ready for taking on a ship.

Early in 1945, the 14,000 ton Cunard liner Ascania came into Buccleuch Dock for the removal of the landing craft which had been fitted for her wartime role as an infantry landing ship. Her original boats and boat davits had to be replaced to convert her into the role of troopship. One task for the repair squad of the Ascania was the removal of some temporary wooden workshops which had been installed on the promenade decks. These were used for the repair and servicing of the ship's landing craft and their engines.

This job was entrusted to Big Norman. Norman was a character who apparently, because of his size and strength, got all the heavy and hard work or humpy jobs which were going. Norman boarded the Ascania with a bag of tools, which included a variety of saws and spanners, over one shoulder. Over the other shoulder was his maul, the 4lb, long-shafted hammer used by all shipwrights, and his favourite tool, a 14lb block hammer. It was not long before the ship resounded to crashing and banging and the splintering of timber. Norman was at work.

Having found that the wooden workshops, complete with work benches and shelves, were securely bolted to the wooden decks and steelwork, Norman decided that a bit of persuasion was necessary to get the job underway. A couple of hours later, when foreman Harry Waterhouse, accompanied by Mr Oughtred, came on the scene, Norman was in the midst of a one-man demolition job. Surrounded by a heap of broken, splintered timber he was busy swinging his block hammer at every piece of wooden structure he could see. Instead of the praise that he expected for his efforts, Norman was told that he was on the wrong deck, knocking down the wrong deckhouses. To say Norman was upset about the situation would be putting it mildly. After all, he had taken the workshops down in record time.

Not only was Norman upset but some of his fellow workmen were too. Two of them had plans to purchase the scrap timber from the workshops to construct a greenhouse. Unfortunately, after Norman's attempts to emulate the proverbial bull in a china shop, or as one shipwright put it: "He was like a wild elephant in a glass factory", the timber was too small to be of use for anything but firewood. Luckily, Big Norman got off the hook the following day. As there was some confusion about the orders given to him, a change of plan was made and it was decided to remove all workshops from all decks.

This time they were removed, or perhaps dismantled is a better word, by the two shipwrights who wanted the timber to build a greenhouse. The job then took somewhat longer than if Norman had been involved. But there again, no one could swing a hammer like Big Norman.

For the record, Ascania had been built at Newcastle in 1925 and gave thirty years of service to her owners and her country before she was scrapped in 1956.

Big Norman's strength was to be put to good use in the repair squad shortly after the workshops incident. HMS Majestic was to be launched on 28 February 1945 and members of the squad, including myself, were given the job of positioning the fenders at Ramsden Dock. These fenders were actually solidly-built floating rafts and, when held in position against the dock walls by ropes, effectively kept the ship's hull away from the wall, preventing damage to either the hull or wall structure.

The fenders were towed down to Ramsden Dock by the yard's firefloat Doris, which acted as a tug and maid of all work in the dock system. To drag these heavy rafts by hand the length of the lock at Ramsden Dock was something of a hard work job, especially if the wind was blowing against you. On occasions they had to be hauled around the outside of ships berthed in the dock. In fact, it could be likened to the scene in the film *Four Feathers* when Lord Kitchener's army was towing its boats up the Nile to relieve Khartoum. Norman, of course, being big and strong, always took the lead position of first man on the rope when towing and positioning the fenders. Needless to say, we always tried to get on the same rope as Norman.

It was on this job that I first came into contact with Tail End Arthur, the man who could always be guaranteed to be carrying the loose or tail end of the rope. Arthur was something of an enigma. He stood out from the rest of his workmates as though he didn't belong, much like the reluctant actor playing a role he was unsuited for and had absolutely no interest in. During the thirty or so years I knew him as a shipwright, he was always a quiet, vague, middle-aged character, entirely unsuited to the rough and tumble of shipyard life. In fact, the part of Sergeant Wilson, played by John Le Mesurier in the TV comedy *Dad's Army*, could have been modelled on Arthur. Each Monday morning he arrived for work wearing clean, neatly-pressed overalls and the shine on his boots would have pleased a drill sergeant in the Grenadier Guards. At the end of the week he was just as immaculate.

When we were engaged on the fender positioning for HMS Majestic, Arthur, in his way, kept us from harm. We had no need to worry about tripping over the loose end of the rope. Arthur had it under full control. No matter how one tried to alter the situation, Arthur always carried the tail end while his mates did the pulling. Similarly, if docking a ship on the floating dock or in the graving dock and heaving on a block and tackle to centralise and hold the ship in position, the tail end was always secure. Arthur would have it wrapped round a bollard. If standing talking in a group on the ship or on the dock wall, Arthur would be on the fringe of the group. Even a casual observer could not help but notice that Arthur always took up the same position on the lee side away from the wind and rain so that his workmates were always sheltering him from the weather. Thus Arthur also obtained the nickname Lee Side Arthur.

Probably, Arthur's only claim to fame was the day he swore back at Big Albert, the foreman. Arthur was in the caulking squad on a liner at the time and the caulking task consisted of hammering oakum or tarry rope between the deck planking seams to make a watertight seal before the seams were filled with pitch. Each tradesman was allocated a certain area, or berth, to complete on the day. The normal berth was 125ft per day. Ten minutes before finishing time, Arthur was sitting on his caulking box preparing oakum for his next day's work. His dreamy faraway gaze proclaimed him to be working out the latest dance steps for his hobby of old time dancing. His reverie was interrupted when Big Albert — sometimes called The Overcoat because he was never off your back — came along and began to test the planking with his knife, to check if the work had been done correctly.

"There's no oakum in there," said Albert.

"Mmmmm," said Arthur.

"What are you going to do about it?" said Albert, his voice like an angry lion.

"Nothing," Arthur said quietly.

"What do you mean, nothing? Why are you going to do nothing about it?" he roared, his voice rising to a bellow that could be heard all over the ship.

"Because it's not my bloody berth," retorted our hero in a slightly irritated tone.

Exit The Overcoat, speechless for once, as were the rest of the caulking squad. Arthur was never known to swear again.

If you were waiting to unload a lorry-load of deck planks or other material, Arthur would be there, standing on the lee side naturally, until the lorry arrived. Then he would go to the toilet. This operation entailed a walk down to the farthest wash place at the end of the dock then a return to the toilets at the other end. Then the procedure was reversed. By the time he arrived back the lorry had been unloaded.

It is a few years since Arthur went to that big shipyard in the sky, but if any shipwright up there ever needs to carry a heavy hydraulic jack, Arthur is sure to be alongside him, carrying the handle.

This story of Tail End Arthur or workmen like him could be told by many shipyard workers from all trades, but on the whole these men were given jobs they could do without problems. Arthur, throughout the years, caulked many feet of wood decking on both liners and tankers and always finished the berth. As Big Norman could swing a hammer, so could Arthur handle a caulking mallet.

To return to the fendering operation.

The day before the launch we had to unload a lorry-load of small or hand fenders at Ramsden Dock. These fenders, made in the spar shed, were simply two 4ft lengths of 9 by 3in stage planking nailed together to form a 6in-thick fender. With ropes at each end, fastened through one piece of planking, the fender was effectively a wooden buffer which could be held by a man on each rope to slide between the ship's hull and the top of the dock wall. In later years, car tyres on the end of a rope were used.

Then came the day of the launch. The records give the date and my memory tells me it was raining. Launches always took place at high water on a spring or high tide, which always reached its peak around noon. Consequently, those engaged in launching and fendering operations always had to bring their own packed lunches and work through their lunch break, grabbing their meals as and where they could. No extra money was paid for this inconvenience as you had normally to finish work an hour earlier. I found out, on this my first involvement with a fendering, launch or docking, that if it rained you got wet.

It is often said that older people always recall that English summers were good and the sun was forever shining. Statistics throughout the years indicate that this was not always the case and that many people tend to remember the happier or sunny days of times gone by.

My own recollections of fendering, launchings and dockings, are just the opposite. It always appeared to be raining, or cold, when we undertook these all-weather jobs. The repair squad, supplemented by shipwrights from other squads, were split into two teams for the fendering of HMS Majestic. One team took the north, or Barrow Island, side of the dock wall, and the other, often smaller, team was allocated the south or town side of the dock system. As luck would have it I was in the south side team where, as the tradesmen explained, there would normally not be so much work. But to counteract that there would be no shelter from the weather.

We were taken down to the Ramsden Dock entrance, or pier head, sitting in the back of a lorry with the rain pouring down. Our route was via St George's Square and down Cavendish Dock Road. Upon arrival at the dock gates we dismounted from the lorry, spread the hand-held fenders around the dock wall and then waited for the launch and arrival of the ship. We had about two hours to wait before the launch and nowhere to go for shelter. The team on the north side had the chance to shelter either in, or in the lee of, the dock gateman's hut or in one of the workshops belonging to the railway company — London, Midland and Scottish, in those days. What made matters worse was that there was no way of getting hot water for a brew. It was a couple of years after the war that the ubiquitous Thermos flask came on the scene.

Our wet weather or protective clothing was virtually any old coat we could get our hands on. Clothing and footwear were on ration and there was no such thing as oilskins in the shops, even if we had the required number of clothing coupons or the money to purchase them. Many workmen, towards the end of the war, wore ex-Home Guard or ex-Civil Defence greatcoats as their heavy weather gear. As can be imagined, once they got really saturated they weighed very heavy and the water soon soaked through overalls and other clothing.

While standing in the rain alongside the lorry (the foreman, of course, was in the cab with the driver) it was decided we would have our dinners before the launch took place and the work commenced. Our food was usually carried, along with the brew cans, in an ex-Army gas mask haversack, 1/6d (7.5p), from the Army and Navy Stores. These were not really waterproof, and unless you were lucky enough to have your sandwiches encased in a tin box or a large square OXO tin, the rain would soak through the haversack into the paper the sandwiches were wrapped in. Today we accept things such as plastic, clingfilm and Cellophane as a matter of course. Had they been around in 1945, life would have been far more comfortable for many people.

Having eaten our soggy sandwiches, standing in the rain, we then saw the launch from afar. I can't remember after all these years if our fenders actually

31

came into contact with the ship as it came through the dock entrance, but no doubt we went through the motions of holding them in position. As the ship was usually carried by the tide and wind on to the north wall it was there that the fenders really came into their own.

Often, if a ship was dragged around the bullnose or corner of the north wall, the 6in-thick fenders positioned between the hull and the coping stones would come under terrific pressure. It was not uncommon for the wood to be compressed from six to three inches and to smoulder and smoke with the friction. Occasionally the shipwrights would be left holding on to a fender-less piece of rope when the wood disintegrated completely. However, it was very rare there was any damage either to the ship, the wall or the workmen.

Once through the dock entrance, 100ft wide in those days, the ship would often tie up in the lock for a time while the outer gates were closed and the water level adjusted to that of the inner dock. While in the lock the ship would normally by lying against the floating fenders.

It was at this stage of the proceedings that we got the opportunity to brew up. The apprentices would collect the brew cans from their mates and if asked politely the crew of the tugs Ramsden and Furness would fill them with the required boiling water. The fendering procedure was repeated as the ship went through the cradle, lifting the railway bridge which separated Ramsden Dock from Buccleuch Dock. The larger ships, such as HMS Majestic, would tie up in Buccleuch Dock for fitting out. Smaller ships such as Hinemoa, Accra and Apapa and the three Peron boats, were fitted out in Devonshire Dock after being fendered through the High Level Bridge. Destroyers also were fitted out in Devonshire Dock. The submarines, of course, further down the dock into their own submarine dock area.

Having possibly at some length given a description of the fendering procedures and conditions in which we worked, perhaps it should be re-corded that fendering, like dockings, were paid at a lesser rate than the normal contract rate. This was probably another reason why many ship-wrights did not view a day's fendering with enthusiasm.

As I recall, the repair squad were on this middle rate of pay all the time, but they did get an allowance of 2/6d (12.5p) dirty money. This was paid if the ship they were working on had been in commission for more than six months. I think the apprentices were allowed 1/6d (7.5p) a week as their dirty money. The lowest rate of pay was the time-rate paid for such jobs as maintenance work on the berths or dock walls.

It was not for about five years after the war that conditions improved for fendering work. At a quarterly meeting of the Shipwrights Union (featured later in a separate chapter), it was announced that the firm had graciously agreed to allow the fendering squads the use of a canvas shelter which could be erected over the back of Vickers lorries. This igloo, as we called it, tied to hooped pipes, did keep the weather off to some extent. A condition of its use was that while it could be fitted to the lorry in works' time, it had to be dismantled after use and stowed in the repair squad store in the users' own time, for which they would not be paid. Ironic cheers greeted this announcement, but at least it was a step in the right direction in the constant quest to improve working conditions. Today I understand it is illegal, under the Health and Safety at Work Act, for anyone to ride in the back of an open lorry.

Over the years, and from the many fenderings in which I participated, two stand out as worthy of mention.

On one occasion a tanker, whose name escapes me, had been completed in the yard and had duly gone out on trials. Instead of commissioning and taking her crew and stores on elsewhere, and returning the trials crew home by train, it was decided that she would return to Barrow for commissioning.

It was a very foggy Sunday lunchtime and the fendering squad and the sailormen squad were stood ready and waiting at the pier head at Ramsden Dock, all geared up for the arrival of the ship. Suddenly her bow loomed out of the fog and we realised that although the tugs were trying to hold her back she was heading straight for the dock wall — and at that speed a collision was inevitable. Three blasts on her whistle was the signal to go astern. The splash of her anchor being dropped and the subsequent rattle of the anchor cable running out showed that the shipwright at the windlass had acted quickly in an attempt to slow the ship down. Unfortunately these actions were just a little bit too late. The tanker's bow hit the coping stones of the dock wall with terrific force. Coping stones were smashed, floodlights on their poles came crashing down — in fact, the earth moved.

Luckily it didn't move as fast as the shipwrights and sailormen. Some, reputably, had cleared the 6ft-high fence in one leap and no doubt records were broken for the hundred yards sprint as the workmen scattered to avoid the crashing debris. Following a count of heads when things had settled down a bit, it was found that no one was hurt. Tail End Arthur was the last to be accounted for, and some said he had been halfway up Ramsden Dock Hill even before the ship hit the wall. However, the tanker was eventually fendered in and tied up in the lock. Her stem was, to say the least, rather bent and twisted and some shell plates were damaged, but again, luckily, no one aboard had suffered injury during the collision.

As we were getting our breath back, and probably brewing up, Mr Redshaw — later Sir Leonard — then the shipbuilding manager, arrived on the scene. His first concern was for the safety of the men rather than the condition of the ship. His spirits were lightened and he burst into laughter, as we all did, after he had spoken to shipwright Paddy McGuire. Paddy, a well known wit, was asked if he was all right.

"Yes," he replied, and pointing to the twisted stem of the tanker, "But it's the first time I've seen a tanker with a hare lip."

Within a week the tanker had her stem repaired, new hull plates fitted, and had sailed away to go about the business she was built for.

The other notable incident concerning the fendering of ships through the dock system occurred in the mid-1950s when the aircraft carrier HMS Hermes went out for trials. Shortly before she was due to leave Barrow it was realised that there could be problems with the clearance through the cradle bridge in Buccleuch Dock.

This problem compounded with Hermes being the first ship to have an angled flight deck, which gave more than the normal overhang adjacent to the underside of the lifting railway bridge. The drawing office came up with an idea to keep the ship away from the bridge by suggesting the construction of a type of timber A frame. Shipwrights constructed this A frame of 12in square logs bolted together, and eventually the structure, about 35ft in length, was transported to the site.

A team of shipwrights from the submarine dock and Devonshire Dock was formed not only to set up the hinges and winches for the operation but also to strengthen the wooden decking below the bridge. Foreman shipwright Big Albert, mentioned earlier, was in charge of the squad and lived up to his nickname of Overcoat as his team worked hard at the various operations.

While a line was being painted on the side of the ship to indicate the correct pushing points, Albert trained his team two or three times a week, stating that he would have them operating like a well-drilled gun team, with everyone knowing his job. The whole operation for the ship's passage through the narrow entrance was to be controlled by blasts on Albert's whistle. Number one winch team would lower away on the winch, number two winch would have the job of raising the frame, or inserting the packing, blocks and wedges as required. The older shipwrights were very sceptical about the whole idea but nevertheless were quite willing to go along with the drill as it made a welcome break from their normal routine.

The day arrived for Hermes to move from her berth where she had lain for so many years that it was suggested she was aground on scrap jobs that had been thrown over her side. However, she gradually moved from the dockside with a flotilla of Liverpool tugs lining up for the cradle bridge entrance. The well-drilled gun team stood at their posts all ready to perform their allotted tasks upon hearing the blasts from their commander's whistle. The A frame was positioned at exactly the right height as the ship began to move through the entrance. At first, Hermes stood over towards the south side and the frame did not touch the shell. But the team worked to the whistle, moving chocks and wedges and following exactly the white painted line on the hull. Albert's report bellowed across the dock to ship manager Archie Baxter.

"She's coming through very nicely, Mr Baxter," was followed by the response: "You wouldna think so if you were over this bloody side." This repartee became a legend among the shipwrights for many a year.

However, back to the A frame.

The tug skippers apparently decided that they could tow the ship faster than the gun team could operate their equipment. Then they either got the ship out of the line or a gust of wind blew her towards the uplifted bridge. To say that things went wrong at this point would be no understatement. Hermes touched the apex of the wooden A frame and within seconds the whole structure bounced out of its hinge points, uprooting winches, packing, logs and wedges before collapsing on the ground like a tree that had been struck by lightning. When the shipwrights surveyed this scene — that by now appeared to look like a firewood merchant's yard — they realised that despite the chaos no one was hurt. Hermes, now three parts through the bridge, was then helped on her way by the traditional fendering method: wooden plank fenders.

Neither Hermes nor the cradle bridge suffered damage during this incident, and when she returned from sea trials she was brought back into the dock with the flight deck overhang on the opposite side to the opening bridge structure. As to the A frame, while the ship was on trials the gun team quietly dismantled all the evidence and tidied up to the extent that no trace of it could be seen.

Probably the idea of the A frame was good, but as the draughtsman who designed it discovered, when a few thousand tons of ship start to get carried along by wind or tide, it takes a lot more than a few 12in thick logs of timber to stop it.

AERIAL view of the Barrow shipyard slipways into Walney Channel

THE launch of the aircraft carrier HMS Majestic, later HMAS Melbourne, on 2 February 1945. I recall that it was raining (photo VSEL)

A BRIDGE too near: HMS Hermes nears the railway bridge which spanned Buccleuch Dock and Ramsden Dock (photo VSEL)

THE "A frame" intended to hold HMS Hermes away from the railway bridge did not really fulfil its purpose (photo VSEL)

IMMEDIATELY after the launch of a ship, the shipwrights erecting squad stage a keel laying ceremony to impress the VIPs on the launch platform and the many spectators. This was showmanship at its best as the steelwork would be removed the following day to allow the berth to be cleared and new keel blocks set up (photo North West Evening Mail)

P&O LINER Chusan under construction in 1947. When a ship was at this stage there were few if any "dry jobs" and it was not unusual for workmen to be sent home without pay until the rain ceased. The ship to the left is the Elder Dempster's Apapa shortly before her launch (photo North West Evening Mail)

Chapter 5

A New Beginning — Post-War Shipbuilders

THE changeover to peacetime shipbuilding in the Barrow shipyard posed no problems for workmen or management. Many of the men who had built the P&O liners Stratheden, Strathmore, etc, and the Orient liners such as Orion and Orcades before the war, were still in the yard. Their skills and expertise were ready to be utilised, and even before the war was officially over some were actually working on the first of the post-war passenger ships.

The Orient Steam Navigation Company had by the time the war ended lost half its fleet of eight ships and new ships were urgently required.

The order for the first ship in the replacement programme was placed with Vickers-Armstrong Limited, as it was then, in March 1945, some months before the conflict was over. Even though the design draughtsmen, naval architects and loftsmen always worked far ahead of the shop floor workers who shape and assemble the steelwork, it was still a good achievement on everyone's part to be able to lay the keel of a 28,470 ton passenger liner on 17 September 1945, only six months after the order was placed.

This ship, Orcades, although being the first post-war ship to be ordered, was not, however, the first ship to be launched after the war. That honour went to the 6,150 ton passenger ferry Hinemoa, which was launched on 30 May 1946 and completed in December of the same year. Looking back for a moment at the times taken to design, build, launch, fit out and complete, to a very high standard, a passenger vessel of any size, illustrates just something of the skills and expertise that existed in the yard in the middle of this century.

Probably the words experience and efficiency are the appropriate words to use when describing what in those days was the normal procedure for a British shipyard. At the top yard the reduced number of A class submarines were becoming ready for launching.

A landing ship, Tank, was under construction on the berth but was only completed to the extent that she was able to be launched, which she duly was in July 1945. She was never fitted out and was scrapped at Ward's shipbreakers.

Work had stopped on the carrier HMS Hermes and the quarter-built hull became a dumping ground for the rest of her steelwork which had been sent out from the platers shed.

Many of the shipwrights normally employed as ironworkers at the top yard were transferred to Devonshire and Buccleuch docks where they sharpened up their woodworking tools to begin the refit of a variety of vessels.

Steam trawlers, which had served their country as escort vessels and minesweepers, were arriving for conversion back to their peacetime role. The Isle of Man steamers needed a refit before their summer season began. Even the humble dredgers and their hoppers, which had kept the port open throughout the wartime years, were in need of an overhaul.

On 5 January 1946 the Barrow-built liner Queen of Bermuda came back to her birthplace for a refit. She was followed into port a few months later by the Orient liner Orion, then later by Stratheden.

Normally, once a ship left Barrow after building she never returned to her birthplace, and it took a world war for the Barrow shipbuilders to have a chance to see again the ships that had given them work and hope during the depression years of the 1930s.

As many of the tradesmen, both engineers and shipbuilders, were engaged on refit work at the dockside, the top yard at the end of 1945 appeared to be relatively quiet. But work increased with the keel laying of Hinemoa and progress on Orcades, which was under construction on Number One berth, formerly occupied by HMS Majestic.

I, along with a number of other apprentices, found myself working on the early stages of construction of Orcades. At this stage I began to take notice of some of the many characters who worked in the yard.

Charlie Harmon (I think I have the name correct) was the leading iron-work foreman shipwright. For many years he carried out this role to the extent that he became a well-known figure to all who worked up the top yard. In his brown overalls (all the foremen wore brown overalls as it was several years later that the firm supplied them with white ones) Charlie would stand on the deck of a ship with never a button fastened and never a coat on his back and give out orders without wasting a word. Yet he always had time for a bit of a laugh with his older workmen and he treated the apprentices fairly. In other words, we seldom got reported to the head foreman for our larking about and our misdemeanours.

Arthur Briley was another shipwright foreman, his nickname cannot be given on account of the Race Relations Act — it began with N and ended in R. The story was told on many occasions of how one of his workmen politely said: "Good morning Arthur." His reply was: "Never mind wasting time discussing the weather, get on with your work."

Foreman shipwright Bill Abbotson — "Bull Abbey" — whose two sons

Charlie and Tommy were both shipwright squad leaders, was what one could describe as a tradesman of the old school. He worked by the book and would sooner send apprentices scouring the top yard for hours searching for used bolts, washers, wedges and chain screws, rather than give out a requisition note, or order, to draw them from the store.

Wilf Burns was the foreman on the submarines and it was always stated that he was quite a nice guy to work for. I found him so, until he got the head foreman's job following the retirement of Tommy Dennis.

Among the older workmen of the time there were also some interesting characters who, with the benefit of long experience, had got the job off to a fine art. Old Taffy Preece, whose son later became head foreman, Billy Reece, Taffy Johns and Old Bob Ashburner — as distinct from his shipwright son Young Bob — were just a few of the top yard personalities of the time.

In the late 1940s there always appeared to be a shortage of the tools and equipment required for the ironwork shipwrights. Long spanners of every size were made in the blacksmiths shop, as were the steel wedges used under a clip to level off the edges of plates, and of course the hydraulic and screw jacks. Other equipment needed was the heavy chain screws and the smaller bottle screws. Instead of the pushing or lifting principles of a jack, the last mentioned items worked in reverse by pulling and holding plates together. Bolts and plate washers were like the items mentioned above, often in short supply, and it was not unusual for the apprentices to try and take these from the riveting squads, when they were not looking, after the riveter had removed the bolts to insert his rivets. This shortage of gear was often attributed to the foreman, who either could not, or would not, order equipment from the stores in sufficient quantities. Where the younger tradesmen shipwrights struggled to acquire the gear to do the job, the old timers always appeared to have an adequate supply of everything.

It was said that these characters could, when staying in the yard for lunch, take a walk around the ship and acquire any such gear that was lying about or not actually in use. The name of Pirates was given to them, not only for their habit of collecting gear but also for their reputed hoarding of it. Some shipwrights reckoned that Old Bob and Old Taffy buried their hoards of gear around the berths, much like the pirates of old did with their treasure. They were reputed to have charts detailing the exact location of their hidden hoards, which apparently read something like: sixteen paces south-west of number six crane, buried, six chain screws, ten spanners and fifty wedges. Or: between the starboard midships bilge blocks of the ship on number three berth. And: hidden, two bags of three-quarter inch bolts, one hydraulic jack and two handles for same. Whether these claims are true or not I cannot confirm, but it is true that these top-class ironwork shipwrights always had plenty of gear — and so in later days did their sons.

Perhaps the charts were passed from father to son. To be fair, though, the pirates, like other tradesmen of the time, never, ever stole gear from their fellow workmates.

It was only in later years when the evils of piecework were applied to the shipwrights trade that wedges and chainscrews would be removed from a job before the welding was completed. This of course meant that the job had to be done again when new gear was acquired. No payment was made for this re-fair as it was called.

In early 1946 the firm decided to revert to pre-war practices for the shipwrights trade. The effect of this apparently simple statement was devastating to those who were affected by it. It meant that when it rained or snowed any shipwright without a dry job could be sent home without pay. When the ships were built plate by plate the shipwrights could be working on the flat or bottom of a tank top for weeks before enough structure was erected to ensure protection from the weather.

Welding, of course, could not be carried out on a wet deck. As many shipwrights were working on the liners Orcades, Hinemoa and later Himalaya, Accra and Apapa, it meant that in bad weather they might be working only one or two days a week with a considerable reduction of money in the pay packet.

Foreman shipwright Bull Abbey was reputed to stand at the bottom of the berth looking down the channel for rain clouds. As the first drops of rain began to fall he would go around his men issuing white pass-outs which effectively sent them home without pay.

Many shipwrights affected by this system said that Bull Abbey seemed to enjoy this task. Some of his older cronies would be given jobs under the bottom of the ship, setting up keel and bilge blocks, but the majority of his men would be sent home. To the younger men, many of whom had just returned from war service, this practice meant real hardship.

After strong representations from the Shipwrights Union the men, after a few months, were issued with yellow pass-outs when it rained. This was some improvement in the respect that although they were still sent home if a dry job could not be found, they got paid a lower time-rate payment. It was several months before this practice of sending men home was finally abandoned, but while it lasted there was much hardship and discontent among the men. The situation was not helped by the fact that it was only the shipwrights who were sent home.

Other trades such as welders, riveters, platers and caulkers, were not affected. Apprentices were not sent home with their mates. They were given another job, under the bottom of the ship or sent to work with the steel erectors hanging up squads. These squads could and did work in the rain as they were not dependent on the welders to get their job done. Only when the cranes could not work owing to gale force winds would the hanging up squads cease their hazardous work.

Although up to now I have concentrated mainly on personalities and characters within the shipwrights trade, there was a host of other tradesmen who will be remembered for being just that little bit out of the ordinary.

The tack welder played an important part in the shipbuilding system. As riveting was phased out and replaced by welding, the shipwrights and platers, instead of bolting the plates together to await the riveters, were obliged to secure their jobs with small intermittent runs of weld. This task was done by a tack welder — as opposed to a piecework welder who would arrive later and weld the whole job completely.

Many of the old riveters, caulkers, holder-ups and platers retrained as tack welders in the welding school for a couple of weeks before being sent out on to the berths to work. Some picked up the job easily and were an asset to the shipwright or plater they were sent to work with. Others took that little bit longer.

If you had to get a bracket welded to hold the weight of a shell plate unit or to withstand the stress and strain and pull of a chain screw, you naturally wanted it to be secured firmly enough to do the job. If it came adrift when the strain came on it you could be in a dangerous situation and the poor tack welder, justifiably, was not always popular. One tack welder, I think his name was Bill, came out on to the berth after his training and as soon as he arrived to work with the shipwrights or platers his opening gambit was: "Is anyone here interested in natural history?"

He got a negative answer. Most of us at the time were far more interested in the fortunes of Barrow Rugby and Willie Horne. Bill's interest was in pre-historic monsters and the words dinosaur, chasmosaurus, parasaurolophus etc would roll off his tongue as fluently as a double-glazing salesman introducing himself on the doorstep. Bill would spend his holidays happily going around the Natural History Museum in London researching these animals, and he no doubt could have been an advisor to Spielberg's *Jurassic Park*.

However, his real claim to notoriety was established in the first few months he was out on the berths. Every time he welded on a bracket, or lug, or tacked a plate in position, he would utter his immortal words: "Will it stick?" For a few months it didn't, no matter how much welding he put on, around or near it. But the name Willit Stick was coined and he carried it with him for the rest of his working life. He later became an expert at his job and mucked in with whoever he was working with. You could always tell where Willit Stick had been working because there was usually a chalk drawing of a dinosaur or some such monster on a nearby bulkhead.

Another tack welder with a great temperament was Bob "Boyo" Dixon from Ulverston. Boyo, whose son Bob was pianist and musical director to the well-known popular comedian and entertainer Max Bygraves, always had a good tale to tell to whoever would listen, and his stories of meeting the London-born entertainer were usually humorous.

As a young tradesman shipwright, I worked mates with John Rigg on and off for several years. John had studied the piano with Boyo's son and therefore had a good relationship with the old tack welder. Often, when tack welders were in great demand on the ships under construction, John could get the services of Boyo solely through this friendship.

One of Boyo's favourite ploys, when working at the forward end of the ship and he had a few spare moments, was to leave his gear and go to the aft end to talk with anyone who would listen. The same applied in reverse if he was working at the aft end. If he was asked to put a few tacks in for someone he would say: "I would come and help you willingly but I'm afraid my gear is at the other end of the ship."

Once John and I had worked out Boyo's pattern we had no trouble. If we found out that his gear was nearby we would take it on to our job and then go looking for the old character at the other end of the ship. Our scheme never failed. As soon as Boyo came out with the offer to help us he was hooked, as John would say: "That's good, we are working at the other end of the ship and your gear is now on our job."

Work on the construction of these big liners and tankers was hard, heavy and dangerous. I think an adage from the noble art of fisticuffs was: "The bigger they come, the harder they fall." Slightly modified it could be applied to shipbuilding in the context: "The bigger they come, the further you fall."

Most of the fatal accidents in the shipyard came from falls on the ships, and at one period statistics proved that the accident rate in shipbuilding was higher than in the mining industry. An old shipbuilding superstition claimed that if a fatal accident occurred to a workman while the ship was being built or launched it would be unlucky throughout its life. But many of the large liners and tankers built in Barrow after the war proved how wrong this was.

Although their construction may have been marred by loss of life, in the main the ships served their owners well without any unfortunate incidents or problems. As far as I can recall there were no fatal accidents on Orcades while she was under construction, but a 21-year-old shipwright, John Irvine, when working with a hanging up squad, was crippled for life when a steel bulkhead fell on him. After all these years the circumstances of this accident are unclear, but probably the fact that the lifting equipment, wire slings, plate grabs, etc, often worn, were not subject to the rigorous inspections and tests of today contributed to this and many other accidents.

When Himalaya was fitting out in Buccleuch Dock a caulker lost his life when testing the mail and store rooms of the ship for leaks. A temporary door blew off its fastenings and, hitting the caulker, knocked him down into the bottom of number two hold. Sadly he was dead before he could be brought ashore.

Later, several accidents occurred during the building of the large oil tankers. One young shipwright's labourer in the hanging up squad had not long been married and welcomed the chance to work on the nightshift for the extra money. In those days there were no floodlights on the berths and the erection of large shell panels was a hazardous enough job by day — but doubly dangerous by night. While working high up on the staging the labourer was presumed to have walked on to what he thought was a stage plank but in reality was only the shadow of one. Apparently, the previous evening there had been a stage plank in that position but it had been removed during the day. The young man fell many feet to his death owing to just one miscalculation.

Many other tragic accidents occurred on the tankers. Most, as stated, were due to falls from staging, but explosions also claimed their victims and not only on the big ships. Many Barrovians will recall how an explosion in the engine room section of HMS Sheffield occurred when she was on the berth and several men lost their lives.

Great damage was caused to the hull and a replacement section was borrowed from the Argentine Navy's destroyer Hercules. The boilermakers at the time worked extremely hard to remove the damaged section of hull and install the replacement. Sheffield was launched on time and through the efforts of the boilermakers the firm was awarded the Queen's Award to Industry. After the award was presented to the firm the shop stewards of the boilermakers were thanked for the efforts of their members over a cup of coffee and two biscuits issued in the manager's offices. The boilermakers yard convenor suggested that the thanks would have been more appreciated if the price of a couple of pints of beer had been put into the pay packets of those who helped win the award. The statement was then made by the firm that the boilermakers should be satisfied by the fact that they had been adequately rewarded by virtue of the extra overtime they had worked.

HMS Sheffield met her end during the Falklands Conflict of 1982, ironically by the very people who only a few years before had offered part of their own vessel to aid her construction. Perhaps the loss of HMS Sheffield resurrected the superstitions of unlucky ships.

But she was just one of the many ships built at Barrow that came to a premature or unfortunate end. The remainder served their owners well without any major incidents, despite some fatalities occurring during their construction period.

One cannot write about accidents in the shipyard without mentioning the name of Vickers ambulanceman and first-aider Bill Quayle. Bill was a caulker/burner by trade and a good one at that. Quite a heavy-built jovial character, he worked as a doorman at the Walney Cinema during the evenings, but it is for his work as an ambulanceman in the yard that he deserves to be remembered. During the accident-prone years of the 40s, 50s and 60s many a workman had cause to thank Bill for his medical expertise.

His ability to size up the extent of an injury, apply first aid, take charge of the situation, particularly in a confined space where access was difficult, was second to none and his orders appertaining to the extrication of a casualty were obeyed without question by staff and workmen alike.

If the previously mentioned tradesmen had a claim to fame there were others who must have a claim to infamy.

As will be gathered by now, the work appertaining to the shipwright's trade was usually heavy and consequently each job was normally a two-man operation. Two shipwrights or a shipwright and a labourer, or a shipwright and an apprentice, was the norm for most jobs. An apprentice could be lucky with the tradesman he worked with. Usually, most of the men were helpful, taught the skills of the trade to the apprentices and treated them well. Naturally there were exceptions.

One tradesman with whom I worked, and who shall be nameless, had his claim to infamy through his attitude to his fellow workmen and his treatment of apprentices. I worked with him on the Elder Dempster passenger liner Accra during the cold winter of 1946-47 and our job included bolting up the decks for the riveting squads.

My tradesman treated his various apprentices, myself included, as if they were slaves. He would never take his turn in going to the stores or platers shed for bolts and plate washers as other tradesmen did. As I recall, the wooden gangway on to the Accra was very long and very steep and the struggle up this stairway to the stars — as it was sometimes called — was bad enough when you had no gear to carry. Carrying a 56lb bag of bolts or plate washers up it four times a day was really hard work. Then to be taken to task by your mate for not hurrying was just one of the things that was not conducive to a happy relationship.

After a few weeks of this soul-destroying, monotonous work with a bad mate, working on the exposed decks in cold winter weather, I asked head foreman shipwright Tommy Dennis for a shift on outfit work. I recall his words as if they were yesterday.

"I want to look after you," he said, "and make you an ironworker. When the hard times come and work is short an ironwork shipwright will get six or eight months work in the year, whereas the outfit shipwright will only get three or four months work in the year. I think it would be better for you to be an ironwork shipwright."

No doubt Mr Dennis was talking from experience and thinking about the pre-war liner buildings such as Strathmore, which was constructed, launched, fitted out and sailing within twelve months. I'm afraid I was not impressed with the thinking and ideas of the head foreman, and with the impetuosity of youth did not look very far into the future. Consequently I asked for a move again at a later date and eventually found myself working on the outfit of the liners with, thankfully, a decent mate.

Before leaving the stories of the top yard tradesmen perhaps the tale of the infamous Scab should be told.

During the early part of the war, in 1940 I think, the shipwrights who, as will be explained later, still had their own union and their autonomy, went on strike for more money. This wartime withdrawal of labour was viewed very seriously and deemed to be traitorous and disastrous to the war effort. However, it lasted less than two weeks and the shipwrights achieved their aim of a decent contract rate of pay.

After only a few days on strike, one shipwright returned to work. Ever after, even until he retired, he was sent to Coventry, ostracised and shunned by his fellow workmates. Apprentices were told by their mates never to lend him any gear or to help him in any other way, under any circumstances. The Scab — very few people used his real name — usually had a labourer working with him because most shipwrights refused to speak to him. I do recall, though, in later years he worked in a hanging up squad. This man was, as far as I know, the only tradesman ever to cross a picket line in the shipyard and one wonders if the treatment he received over the years served as a deterrent to any other would-be strike breaker.

THE Shipwrights trial squad aboard Orsova in 1954. Back row left to right: Arthur Patrick, George Corkhill, Eric Kendall. Middle row: Andy McVeigh, Wesley Raynor, Alec McGrady, foreman Bob Munroe, Arthur Barker, liner-off George Cottam. Front row: Albert Jenkinson, apprentice Jack Sargent, Paddy McQuire, the author, labourer Jim McBride (photo author)

PRESIDENTE Peron, one of the three smart liners built for the Argentine government (photo North West Evening Mail)

ORCADES leaving Sydney on 15 November 1950, a sight that will never be repeated (photo author)

DURING the launch of the P&O liner Chusan, the starboard forward launch cradle collapsed as she slid down the ways. Despite taking a list to starboard she suffered no damage. The photo shows how all the timber launchways and stilts came away from under the ship as she listed back to port (photo VSEL)

THE end of an era and a beautiful ship. Orsova at the breakers yard exactly 20 years after her maiden voyage (photo P&O)

Chapter 6

The Launching and Outfitting of the Liners

BY THE time the winter of 1946-47 was over most of the shipyard tradesmen had returned home from war service and it was soon noticeable that the standard uniform in the yard had changed somewhat.

Instead of the ubiquitous flat cap and blue overalls worn for so many years the ex-servicemen introduced a new fashion in work clothing. The battle dress blouse, khaki for the Army and Home Guard, coupled with the navy blue of the Civil Defence, became standard dress for the returned servicemen and those who had served in the part time organisations on the home front. The flat cap was replaced by the service beret and it was not unusual to see a shipyard worker dressed entirely in khaki or navy blue uniform, less badges of rank of course. Even the Air Force blue tunics were seen on occasions.

Probably those who served in the Royal Navy were unlucky. Despite the new fashions in work clothing, which lasted until the uniform was worn out, I cannot recall seeing anyone wearing a seaman's tunic or bell-bottom trousers. Obviously this rig did not lend itself to crawling around in the double bottoms of ships or the laying of wood decks.

I mentioned earlier that the training programme for apprentices in those early post-war years was virtually non-existent.

However, there were night school classes for shipwright and plater apprentices. Apparently, few apprentice shipwrights had been attending these evening classes and I think at the time there were only two apprentice platers in the yard. Shortly before evening classes were due to commence in September 1946, all the apprentice shipwrights were summoned to the office of the then shipyard manager, Bob Nicholson.

The advantages of going to evening classes were stressed by both Mr Nicholson and our head foreman, Tommy Dennis. The 15-20 lads in their first, second or third years of apprenticeship were not impressed by this soft sell and we showed little, if any, enthusiasm for the prospect of attending night school two evenings a week. Then the soft sell approach became a bit more serious, with veiled hints about how those with the night school experience would be kept on in the yard when the hard times came.

We began to think up excuses for not attending classes. Apprentice Joe Largue put before Mr Nicholson what we thought was a cast-iron excuse.

"Just can't afford to go," he said. "The money you pay us in wages is not enough to keep the cat in milk let alone sufficient to buy drawing boards, tee-squares and pencils."

Mr Nicholson smiled and then played his trump card.

"That's no problem," he said. "I will have the drawing boards and tee-squares made in the joiners shop and they will be kept for you, along with pencils, at the school."

We had no further excuses to put forward and consequently enrolled for evening classes in Ship Details and Scrieve Loft. These classes took place on Tuesday and Thursday evenings from 7-9pm in the then Barrow Technical School in Abbey Road. Our teacher was George Blair, an old Scottish ships draughtsman, and despite our high spirits and somewhat unwillingness to learn he did keep us under control, after a fashion, and taught us the rudiments of the trade.

The scrieve loftwork consisted of laying out plywood boards in the school gymnasium and scrieving in, cutting in with a special knife the body view of a ship, as was practice in the yard's Mould Loft. Ship details included the drawing of ship sections to scale. This part of the course also included the details and spacing of rivets.

I'm afraid that my attitude to this latter part of the course was much the same as when at Barrow Grammar School, during French lessons, I said: "If a Frenchman wants to speak to me let him learn English."

When I told George Blair that riveting, in my opinion, would soon be a thing of the past and that we did not need to know about rivets and riveting, he took it quite calmly. In his mild way, with a quiet Scots' accent, he said: "As you go through life you never know just what information will be of benefit to you. What you learn now could possibly help you to keep a job in later years."

I had cause to thank both my French teacher and George Blair in later years.

When I was assistant carpenter for the Orient Line the verb "ferme", French for close, came back to me, and by its use, when taking aboard water in Cherbourg, I was able to get the French waterman to close a valve and thus prevent a flooding of the first class dining salon.

As regards the rivets. Some twenty or so years after my night school training I was working as a loftsman in the Mould Loft and given a plan for an all-riveted mast for a destroyer. Amazingly, my memory recalled the basic spacing for rivets and I was able to complete the job without too much trouble.

However, having digressed somewhat, I, like most of the other apprentice shipwrights and the two apprentice platers, did my two years at night school and obtained first-class distinctions in both subjects. Looking back, I think Mr Blair could have been slightly over generous when marking our exam papers, which he set, but the reward for our attendance and the passing of the exams was worth the effort.

A pass at distinction level brought a payment of £4. This figure today may seem an insignificant sum but when, as a third-year apprentice, I was earning £1.10s (£1.50) for a 42-hour week, a gift of £4 was well worth having. To make another comparison, one week's full board and lodging at that time was £1.15s (£1.75).

But back to the ships.

The job of an outfit shipwright included the installation and testing of almost everything which went on the outside of a vessel. This took in winches, derricks, masts, lifeboats, anchors, gangways, wood decks, handrails, stanchions and a myriad of other jobs. On the inside of the vessel the work included the fitting out of holds, hatches, magazines on naval vessels, the installation of machinery seatings and auxiliary machines such as refrigeration and air-conditioning units. Eyeplates, ladders and lifts were also part of the job of an outfit shipwright. The laying of wood decks was an arduous, time-consuming task, but, like all the other outfit jobs on the liners and later on tankers, provided much job satisfaction.

I found this varied work on outfit much more to my liking than the top yard work of an ironworker. At least on outfit work one had the chance to use one's many woodworking tools on occasions and in many cases to follow the job through from start to finish. A close-working relationship existed between the outfit shipwrights and the tradesmen from other departments. Such examples could be found when the shipwrights fitting the boat winches, davits and lifeboats worked with the ship riggers in the reeving-off of lifeboat falls and the testing of the whole job.

Shipwrights and blacksmiths also enjoyed a working relationship. One shipwright I worked with as an apprentice, by the name of Billy Brooks, lifted measurements and made templates for all the ladders and stairways on Orcades, in addition to fitting all the stanchion supports for the guard rails. As these items were all made in the blacksmiths shop he, and I as his apprentice, spent some time in the ship smithy taking in templates and then taking delivery of the finished items.

The ship smithy was a busy department with its own head foreman, Charlie Lupton, its own foreman, chargehands, marker-offs, fitters, welders and drillers, in addition to about fifteen blacksmiths and their strikers or helpers. In all about 120 people.

At the end of the war the blacksmiths were based in the old platers shed near the shipyard gate at the top yard. The floor where they worked was composed of earth. There were open coke fires and no extractor fans to remove the coke and sulphur fumes. Consequently, conditions were deplorable, not only for the blacksmiths but also for those who worked nearby. The blacksmiths and their strikers always had a pint mug of tea alongside their fires and it was noticeable that the mug was always covered with a tin lid to keep out the all-pervading dust and fumes.

Shortly after the war the ship smithy was moved to Buccleuch Dock into a purpose-built shop where conditions were much improved. Over the years the blacksmiths department was run down and combined with the boiler dock department and the ship platers department.

Now this once-busy department, with its skilled blacksmiths has like many other shipbuilding departments and trades, disappeared completely and is just a memory to some of the older retired tradesmen. But some evidence of their existence is still visible. In 1991, when I left the yard, it was still possible to see, on the sandstone walls of Number One bay in the assembly shop, the soot, smoke and sulphur stains caused by the open fires of almost fifty years ago.

The contacts made by the outfit shipwrights with other tradesmen stood them in good stead throughout the years, and mutual help, advice and assistance between tradesmen and their foremen was always to hand when called for.

In what could be called the prime years of post-war liner construction — 1946 to 1954 — many fine ships were built, and arguably the best looking ones and the happiest to work on were the three passenger cargo liners for the Argentine government, known to the workforce and the Peron boats. The three ships, Presidente Peron, Eva Peron and 17 du Octubre, were happy to work on and there was always a good atmosphere among the workmen.

One incident comes to mind after all these years. In Devonshire Dock, one of the ships, I forget just which, was nearing completion and furniture was being brought aboard by the joiners and their labourers. As we sat, one fine evening, on the aft end of one of the promenade decks having our tea break, a baby grand piano was unloaded and left on the deck. The joiners and their labourers, late for their tea break, rushed ashore intending to move the instrument later. The shipwrights of the day were nothing if not versatile and curious to boot. John Rigg, who later became a great long-time mate of mine, was, as I mentioned in a previous chapter, a pianist of some repute. Being the character that he was John, who at the time was working on the deck planing machine, just could not resist the temptation to admire the beautiful new piano. To his amazement and delight the keys to the instrument were in view and secured only by a piece of Sellotape.

"Just one little tinkle on the ivories," said John as he opened the lid. After a few bars of music which included a popular tune of the day and an impassioned rendering of *Pinetops Boogie Woogie,* which attracted much applause from his audience of shipwrights, he was asked for a request number. Now Arthur Barker, a fellow shipwright, was a keen dancer. Not just an ordinary dancer but a master of ceremonies at local dances who danced every night of the week. His speciality was ballroom dancing.

"Play *Moonlight and Roses,*" he told John, "while I demonstrate these new dance steps."

With Lee Side Arthur as his partner the two men began to perform some fancy dance steps. A shout of "What the hell's going on here?" halted the piano player, the accompanying singers and the dancers, mid-stride exactly as if they were playing a game of charades. The ship's manager, accompanied by what appeared to be a dozen Argentine admirals and generals sporting yards of gold braid and followed by several immaculately dressed ladies, stood staring in amazement at the tableau of shipwrights gathered around the piano. Expecting at least a week's suspension if not dismissal, we started to move sheepishly away to escape the wrath that was surely to follow. But the tension was broken by the laughter of some of the ladies in the party and soon the whole party of VIPs were joining in. The VIP party moved into the lounge and then continued what was, apparently, a tour of the ship.

Then the next day saw the culprits assembled outside the manager's office at 9am. We trooped in expecting the worst as we saw our foreman, head foreman, ship's manager and two Argentine officers seated across the table from us as if a court martial had been convened. Two minutes later we were all outside again clutching four cartons of American cigarettes between us and all mightily relieved to have got away with only a warning.

The story of our impromptu concert soon got around the shipyard along with the assumption that the lady who led the party was actually Eva Peron herself, the wife of the Argentine President Peron, whose story has been told in the Lloyd Webber musical *Evita*. It is on record that Evita never came to Britain, but, who knows, perhaps she visited Barrow incognito.

Many of the shipwrights who had served in the forces during the war worked on these Peron boats as they were being fitted out in Devonshire Dock. Big Johnny was one such shipwright and it did not take much persuasion to get him talking about his experiences in the Army.

In our foreman's office at Devonshire Dock were stored an old .303 rifle and a Thompson Tommy gun. These weapons were used for trying out the stowage and gun racks in the small arms magazines on warships. The guns could in no way be made to fire as they were minus bolts and triggers. The rifle was a .303 Short Lee Enfield Mk V and was Big Johnny's favourite. I knew the type and make exactly, as did the other apprentices, because Johnny told us often enough. If we stayed for our dinners, which we ate in the store,

59

one word about the war or the armed forces was sufficient for Johnny to get out the rifle. Then followed a lesson in rifle drill as Johnny marched around the store shouting out orders to himself. After this exhibition of small arms drill, which would not have disgraced a foot soldier in the Brigade of Guards, Johnny would announce he was conversant with the gun because he had been a sergeant musketry instructor to which he never failed to get a response from one of his captive audience.

"How can you know all about rifles if you had muskets in your regiment? I thought they went out of fashion a long time ago."

This standard question would infuriate Big Johnny, who would then talk about the ranks and traditions prevailing in the British Army.

All good fun and it did pass the time away during our dinner hour.

In those days there was, in the main, only one ship manager and one foreman from each department allocated to each ship. The joiners, though, and sometimes the electricians, had several foremen on each ship, particularly the larger liners.

Shipwright outfit foremen were Billy Strong and Bob Munro. Billy Strong was, at first impression, an easy-going foreman to work for. If he walked into the store and some of the men were late in jumping to their feet or acknowledging him (this procedure was normal for the time) he would smile and say: "Don't get up, it's OK." But if this happened on a couple of occasions the regular offenders would find themselves in his bad books. They could be shifted up to the top yard, given a task job such as deck caulking, placed on the next docking or fendering list, for less money, or they were not asked to work overtime for a couple of weeks.

Strangely, it was never foreman Billy Strong who imparted the bad news to his men, this task was always allocated to his contract leader/squad leader Arthur Turner. Billy Strong retained his nice guy image because, after say a couple of offending apprentices had been in the caulking squad for a few days, depending on the severity of the offence, he would walk past them on the deck then halt in his tracks. With a surprised look on his face he would then say: "I didn't know you were in the caulking squad. You had better go back to work with your mate in the morning."

Because of actions such as this he was always reckoned to be too good to be true as he never gave out any bad news. But it must be said that every apprentice who worked under him learned one part of the trade thoroughly — how to caulk a deck.

Bob Munro, the other outfit foreman, was always decent with his men and apprentices. He often put two apprentices together, much to their delight. After all, it could get rather boring if you worked with an older man for months at a time.

Working mates with another lad of the same age meant that it was possible to have a bit of a laugh and a joke while still getting on with the job.

I recall that Jim Johnson and myself laid the first-class dance floor on Himalaya. This deck was of teak and a lighter coloured wood — I forget just which — and when it was caulked and the seams payed up with white pitch we were quite proud of our efforts. Naturally, while working on this job, some of the tradesmen working nearby kept a watchful eye on us as did the liner off, Arthur Hepworth.

Other apprentices working together were laying deck on the bridge areas. Although there was not actually competition and rivalry between the apprentice squads, a hint was occasionally dropped that the two lads on the bridge were making a good job and appeared to be laying a lot of deck. Such a hint was often taken and spurred us on to working that little bit harder.

Caulking the decks, as described earlier, was a task job but not all of the wooden decks on a liner were caulked by hand. The hand caulking was mainly undertaken in the confined areas such as between the bollards or boat davits or close to the deck edges. The open areas of deck were caulked with the caulking machine. This device consisted of a heavy four-wheeled steel frame on which was mounted a large electric motor. This motor drove an eccentric crank which, in turn, lifted a wide caulking iron, or chisel, up and down with great force. A roll of thick heavy oakum, like tarry rope, was, once the machine was positioned, fed into the seams and driven deep into the space between the planking. The whole device was driven along by its controlling shipwright while his apprentice guided the oakum. Once at the end of its run the machine would be levered out of its caulked seam and pushed across the deck to its new seam and the whole procedure would begin again. Two threads of machine oakum were driven in by the machine whereas the hand caulkers hammered in three threads.

During the fitting out of a liner the chirping ring of the hand-caulking mallets — each mallet had its own individual sound — the heavy thump, thump of the caulking machine and the whining screech of the planing machine, could be heard as far away as Barrow town centre.

The planing machine was used to level off and smooth the decks when caulking was finished and was basically a version of an extremely heavy lawn-mower. Even though the heavy electric motor drove the razor-sharp steel blades, the machine still had to be pushed. At the end of a day's work on the planing machine the operating shipwright had certainly earned his money.

An apprentice always worked with the man on the planing machine. It was the lad's task to wet down the deck with buckets of water to prevent the pitch sticking to the plane blades and also to sweep clear the shavings. One character from the days of the caulking machine was old Albert Pogson.

Albert, reputed to be well into his seventies, was usually employed as a jobbing caulker. In effect he had the task of caulking around the scuppers and the butts in front of the caulking machine. These butts, as they were called, were where the deck plank ends joined, and of course they had to be caulked and payed up with pitch.

Old Albert was a familiar sight on the liners, hunched up on his caulking box swinging his caulking mallet with the expertise gained over many years. Even though smoking on the ships fitting out was an offence, punishable by instant dismissal, Albert always had a cigarette dangling from his lips. He coughed and spluttered but he never faltered in his rhythm except to light another cigarette. Albert was reputed to smoke fifty Capstan Full Strength cigarettes a day and he probably did. How he never got the sack for smoking, no one ever knew, but perhaps he was such a familiar sight around the decks that the manager and foremen did not notice the clouds of smoke and the pile of cigarette stubs that surrounded him.

As I served my apprenticeship, like many other shipwright lads I went down on the launch of one or two ships. The most dramatic launch that I recall was that of the P&O liner Chusan. Her keel was laid in February 1947 and a novel feature of her building was the arc of plating cut from her stem to allow the railway engines to pass underneath. However, modernisation of the shipyard was well underway and the section of stem plating was welded back once the railway track had been moved. Chusan was launched on Tuesday 25 June, 1949, and only two months before this date the decision had been made to install Denny-Brown stabilisers into her, making her the first liner to have such equipment. From a launching point of view she was also the first Barrow ship to be fitted with internally released drag chain slips. Understood to be a design of Sir Leonard Redshaw, these release chain slips were a great success and were used until the last launch into Walney Channel.

As an apprentice my job was to be stationed in the lower decks adjacent to number three hold, there to answer the telephone and to pass the orders, as and when, to release the drag chain slips. Chusan's launch was nothing if not dramatic.

As she got about half-way down the slipway, and the weight began to be transferred to her forward launch cradle, the starboard cradle began to collapse and she listed over to starboard before she was finally afloat.

Down below, in the semi-darkness of the 'tween decks, I, and the shipwrights standing by the drag slips at the shell side, felt the ship begin to list and heard the crashing and banging as loose gear such as the joiners' plywood bulkheads fell over and plumbers' pipes began to roll down to the starboard side. Some of the shipwrights had to jump out of the way as the pipes rolled down towards them — but miraculously no one was hurt.

Once afloat, Chusan rolled back to port and all the starboard launchways floated free. Orders came down the telephone, the drag slips were released and the foremen checked there were no injuries.

The collapse of the launch cradle was reputably due to a fire which had occurred in the cradle poppets only a few days before, and there had been insufficient time to replace the damaged timber.

Shortly after the launch, when Chusan was fitting out, those of us working in the holds were surprised to find the double-bottom tanks in numbers one and two holds had been filled with water ballast. As this was not usually a common practice for launching, some people held the theory that this additional weight had contributed towards the collapse of the launch cradle.

An interesting footnote to this incident occurred when the Vickers fire brigade slung a portable fire pump into number two hold with the intention of emptying the tanks of the water ballast. Apparently, the power of this petrol-driven pump was insufficient to lift the water from the tanks so the pump was left in situ for a few months. When the pump was eventually removed from the hold and landed on the dockside the fire brigade had a surprise awaiting them. To their astonishment the complete engine had been removed and, in short, the pump unit was in place but, like Old Mother Hubbard's cupboard, the engine compartment was bare. It was said, in later years, that one of the best lifeboat conversions on Walney Channel was the one that sported a four-cylinder petrol engine of exactly the same make as the one that had been in the fire brigade trailer pump.

The water was eventually removed from Chusan's tanks by the use of compressed-air pumps.

Shortly before Chusan was due to leave Barrow for sea trials, orders came from the drawing office that she had to have additional ballast in her forward holds to get a correct trim. To this end concrete blocks once used as anti-tank traps during the war were dumped into numbers one and two holds. If my memory is correct there were approximately 100 tons in number one hold and 150 tons in number two hold. Steel tubes were situated to give access to the tanks then chippings were dumped around the blocks and the whole lot concreted over.

My mate Dennis and I were the two shipwrights involved in the fitting of shuttering boards on this job, much to the dismay of the shipyard joiners who, under their delegate Alderman George Hastwell, had claimed the job. However, the shipwrights won the day and in early June 1950 the Chusan, complete with her concrete ballast, left Barrow for Liverpool then later for sea trials on the Clyde.

Looking back over the years one wonders if the Vickers naval architects had made an error in their calculations which necessitated the installation of additional ballast in the Chusan.

Chusan served her owners well for more than 20 years, but one cannot help but wonder if, when the Taiwanese shipbreakers began their gruesome work on her in 1973, they called in a navvy gang to remove the concrete from the holds.

Chapter 7

Shipbuilders at Sea

MY APPRENTICESHIP as a shipwright was completed in December 1949 when I had served a total of five years and three months. The extra three months were added on to make up for time lost during the normal five-year period of apprenticeship. Under the conditions prevailing at that time I was not entitled to a full tradesman's rate until I was 21. Consequently, I was paid at an improver's rate for the three months until I had reached the age of maturity. The wage was £4.18s (£4.90) which was £1 a week less than the craftsman's rate.

Although I came out of my time working on the outfit of Chusan I had been on sea trials of Himalaya during the summer of 1949. This experience strengthened my ambition to get away to sea as a ship's carpenter.

When a ship, particularly a large passenger liner, was nearing completion at Barrow the town enjoyed something of a mini boom. Contractors such as the famous furniture firm of Waring and Gillow sent their men to fit out the luxurious dining and public rooms. Contract painters were often drafted in to help out the local tradesmen, and squads of ashphalters, lino layers and carpet fitters were a common sight onboard. All these spent their money in the town.

The association between the men who built the ships at Barrow and the men who sailed in them has always been very close, and many of the local men who worked on the construction of the Vickers built liners often started new careers by serving in them in various capacities.

During the building of the P&O Orient liners, both pre and post-war, heads of the departments of shipping companies would have a spell in the town, supervising at first the hull construction then later the fitting out and victualling of the ship before it left for trials. During their stay in Barrow, which varied from a few months to a year, these marine superintendents, engineers, electricians, hull overseers and later the stewards and store-keepers, would stay in the local hotels and boarding houses. Many friend-ships were made between the local people and the shipping company officials, some of which lasted for many years.

When a liner was in the last stages of fitting out, drafts of stewards would arrive to load aboard mattresses, linen, cutlery, food and the thousands of items that were required to transform a part-completed ship into a fully operational luxury liner. Perhaps many Barrovians smelled for the first time the pungent aroma of curry when the Indian and Pakistani deck and engine room crews of the P&O liners started cooking their own food aboard.

On the Orient liners the crew were all European. It was not uncommon for some of the crew members standing by their ship to meet up with some of the local girls and eventually marry them.

During the final stages of fitting out, an air of expectancy pervaded the town and the shipyard. The stewards and seamen enjoyed their spell ashore and lived life to the full. The local pubs were packed every night and the ships' crews learned the words of *The Boys of Old Barrow*, a song that kept its popularity with the Orient Line and was sung at most Sunday night crew concerts when the ship was at sea. Indeed, during my time with the Orient Line I heard the local song sung in many clubs, pubs and ports all over the world. In return, the crews in pubs such as The Wheatsheaf, Duke of Edinburgh, Kings Arms, Snipe and Bull, taught the local lads *The Orient Line* song and one entitled *One Day I went to the Fair.*

Of course, in those days any pub that called itself a pub had to have a singing room with its local personalities. Andy Ross and Johnnie Worthington, both shipyard characters in their own right, were well known attractions at the Big Cav — the Cavendish hotel in Dalton Road.

In the yard, the talk was of sea trials where the prospect of a working voyage on the ship was the goal. Apprentices went on the job that little bit earlier and worked that little bit harder. Journeymen, too, were more polite to their foremen. All this was in the hopes of a break from routine and the chance to earn some extra money at sea.

After the many farewell parties, on the eve of sailing the crew would join the ship. The chosen few lucky ones among the shipyard workers would already be aboard on the eve of departure, standing watches and getting into the routine of shipboard life, albeit for a week or ten days. On departure day thousands of people would be at Ramsden Dock and Roa Island to wave their goodbyes to the ship that they would probably never see again.

My first voyage was on Himalaya with foreman shipwright Bob Munro and two tradesmen, Arthur Hepworth and George Corkill. For some reason the normally very placid shipyard joiners, who never had the reputation of being on the militant side, decided to have a ban on overtime. Consequently, about twenty apprentice joiners were taken on sea trials with three foremen joiners to keep them in hand.

I recall that Himalaya went into the Thompson graving dock at Harland and Wolff's Belfast yard for her hull to be cleared of the remaining launch cradle structure, then a propeller overhaul and bottom painting.

Our accommodation on trials was luxurious. The food, after years of rationing, was fantastic, and to cap it all we were given two bottles of beer each day at the lunch table. We were accommodated in the tourist class section of the ship, ate in the tourist dining saloon, and were looked after by the Goanese stewards.

The only trouble was that there was always a lot of work to do and the hours — both at sea and in port — were long. We worked from 7.30am until 9pm most days, although during our two days stay in Belfast we were allowed ashore one evening at 7.30pm.

After successful completion of sea and speed trials on the Clyde we were given a present of two extra bottles of beer. All too soon our sea voyage was over and we returned home, from Southampton, to the reality of shipyard life.

Several Vickers tradesmen had successful careers at sea before returning to the shipyard. On board Himalaya, making their first voyages, were plumber Ken Cresswell, shipwright Lance McCarten, sailing as assistant carpenter, and shipwright Jim Parker, sailing as a utility steward. Several other local men sailed aboard the ship as junior engineers or electricians.

Getting away to sea in the 1950s was not always easy. Engineers and electricians, along with stewards, always appeared to be in demand. But for shipwrights and joiners wishing to sail as carpenters it was a bit of a *Catch 22* situation.

The shipping companies, when approached, would say: "Get a note from the Shipping Federation (commonly known as The Pool), and we will give you a job." The Shipping Federation, when approached, would say: "Get a note from the shipping company and we will put you on The Pool."

Having tried for several months to get away to sea at my trade, I, and fellow workmate Dennis Waites, eventually joined the P&O company as stewards. After a four-month voyage to Australia and back aboard the P&O Maloja — working a ten-hour day, seven-day week for the princely sum of £17.10s. per month — we returned home with a seaman's discharge book. This was our passport to The Pool and the key to getting employment as assistant carpenters.

There is not much to say about this voyage aboard an old liner carrying British emigrants to Australia, except that sea going was far removed from shipyard life. Only about forty white stewards were carried aboard the Maloja, the remainder of the catering department, except for leading cooks etc, were Goanese.

Our immediate supervisor was the third steward, a genial, jovial, Pickwickian type of character reputed to have been a former concert pianist with a famous London orchestra. Our job was to wait on the forty or so white stewards, lay tables, serve the food and generally clean up their quarters.

Berthed in a cabin with six other stewards, our quarters were, to say the least, not very spacious or comfortable. In the cabin there were four double bunks, two on each side, eight tin lockers serving as wardrobes, and a mirror on the back of the door. There was also one portlight and two punkah-louvre vents to give us a form of ventilation.

On sailing night, when we had finished serving supper and we were ready to get in our bunks, we had a visitor. A tall blond, immaculately groomed bedroom steward with the features of a Greek god came into the cabin, lifted his leg up with a high kick and — placing his foot on the overhead beam — introduced himself as Deidre and offered to kiss us all goodnight. Suffice to say that persons like this did not exist in Barrow or if they did they were most certainly unknown to us. Politely refusing Deidre's offer, we came to the conclusion that we were in for an interesting voyage.

Maloja, built in Belfast in 1925, carried 1,030 passengers in one class following her post-war refit. Their accommodation was not over-luxurious but the object was to get the assisted passage emigrants to Australia to start a new life.

The saloon waiters with whom we sailed were nearly all young lads and full of fun. When serving the meals to the passengers the young stewards competed with each other to see who could finish first. I recall that one steward claimed a record for carrying — at one time without a tray — fourteen plates of soup and serving them to his passengers without spilling a drop.

Homeward bound, after leaving Bombay where many of the Indian, Pakistani and Goanese crew were paid off and replacements taken on, the third steward took his own life by jumping over the side. After he was reported missing at the second sitting of breakfast, Maloja was put on a reciprocal course and a four-hour search instigated. No trace of him was ever found. An atmosphere of doom descended over the ship and we were glad to arrive at our home port of Tilbury.

It could be said that seagoing life was completely divorced from and entirely different to anything we had experienced in our home town.

Once we were paid off from Maloja with our seaman's discharge books, the way was clear to apply for the position of assistant carpenter. Despite our lowly status and inexperience during this voyage on Maloja, when giving in our notice we were asked to stay on the ship and offered promotion to assistant stewards. Dennis stayed with the P&O company and sailed as an assistant carpenter. I was able to obtain a similar position with the Orient Line and after a few weeks at home went back to Tilbury to join Orcades.

Although this book is written in an attempt to portray life in the Barrow shipyards, this inclusion of seagoing life and personalities serves to make a comparison between two very different worlds and employers.

The Orient Line was a very good employer and treated everyone, from the highest to the lowest, with equal respect and consideration. In the 1950s all seamen were entitled to a £1 per month rise for every year of sea service up to a maximum of four years. When signing articles for a voyage — normally three months to Australia and back — the company official would ask if you were eligible for such a rise. If a rise was due at any date during the voyage, the extra money would be paid from the date of signing on. Such considerations would never have occurred in the shipbuilding industry where no workman ever got a penny more than he was entitled to.

After three years service with the Orient Line all sea-going personnel from captain down to the humble scullions, plate washers and potato peelers, were offered a company contract. Such a contract meant extra money, continuous pay whether at sea, on leave or paid off sick, security of employment and extra leave. The Orient Line, and I believe other shipping companies, adopted this policy on the basis that if you were good enough to work for the company for three years it was worthwhile for the company to offer you better conditions in order to keep your services.

Such a contract was equivalent, or even well above, the staff conditions enjoyed by some Barrow shipyard employees, the main difference being that the shipping company gave the status and conditions to the person, whereas staff conditions in shipyards were applicable to the job.

One other example of Orient Line employee relations was the custom of distributing long service awards. These were presented to eligible crew members at a cocktail party on the ship on the evening prior to sailing day. The awards consisted of the presentation of a silver badge in the form of a Roman numeral for every five years of service. For the first five years the recipient would receive his badge V and £5. When ten years had been served a ten year badge X was awarded along with the sum of £10. Some crew members even had their 40-year badges.

Appreciation of the crew's service by awards certainly helped the shipping companies to obtain and keep a loyal and experienced workforce in all departments. In contrast one can only say that employment in the shipbuilding industry of Great Britain was always classed as casual labour.

The Orient Line was also noted for being one of the few companies that remembered its personnel during the war years. My father-in-law, Frank Tolley, an ex-shipyard plumber, was serving as first plumber on the Barrow-built liner Orama when she was sunk by enemy action in the North Sea. On each of the five Christmases that he and his fellow seamen spent in a German prisoner of war camp, the company sent them a Christmas card in addition to contributing generously towards Red Cross parcels. On their return home the company gave Orama's crew substantially more than their due emoluments.

This digression from the main theme of the book is probably sufficient to illustrate the different ways in which shipbuilders and shipowners treated their personnel.

With the rank of petty officer aboard Orcades, I found conditions much improved from that of a steward aboard the Maloja. A two-berth cabin, a deck boy to clean it and change the linen, dining in the leading hands mess on tourist-class food with Saturday afternoons and Sundays off, except for essential work, was a great way to see something of the world, particularly as I was getting paid for it.

Orcades was a happy ship and during my time aboard her I sailed with Barrow plumbers Fred Rawlings and Bob Midwood. Other local men aboard were third electrician Jack Liddell and quartermaster Jack Davenport. In addition were several Barrovian stewards. My fellow assistant carpenter was a shipwright from the Isle of Wight. He was very proud of having served a seven-year apprenticeship as a boatbuilder and shipwright with the firm of J Samuel White under a head foreman by the name of James Foster. By a strange coincidence, and being a small world, I was to meet the latter-mentioned person at a later date, as will be told in a further chapter.

The work of an assistant carpenter at sea was nothing if not varied. In addition to the general maintenance of the ship our everyday chore was to sound or measure the amount of fresh water in the tanks, morning and afternoon. We were also responsible for taking aboard the fresh water while in port. Other work included such jobs as erecting the stalls for the passengers' funfair.

This funfair was just one form of entertainment laid on for the passengers, both first class and tourist. The stalls were operated by the stewards and all profits went to the crew's social and benevolent fund. I can also lay claim to designing and making a sleigh for the arrival of Santa Claus at the children's Christmas party.

Perhaps the most unusual job I was ever given was the task of making a coffin for a pet monkey. This chore was undertaken at the request of the crew who, owing to quarantine regulations, were not allowed to bring their friendly, mischievous pet into England. The poor monkey was measured up when still alive, and the coffin was duly constructed of varnished mahogany plywood, suitably weighted of course. On the evening prior to our arrival in Tilbury the pet was consigned to the deep after the dispenser had administered the *coup de grace* with the requisite injection.

After a spell serving in Orcades I came ashore to get married and to work again in the Barrow shipyard. Before leaving the ship I was offered the chance to return to the company at any time in the future.

When I applied for a job back in the yard, Mr Wilf Burns, the head foreman shipwright, and although there was plenty of work available, carried out his usual policy of keeping prospective employees on the dole for a few weeks before sending for them. Once back in the yard I worked on both iron work and outfit on the bauxite ore carrier Carl Schmedeman. It was on this ship I worked mates with shipwright John Rigg and began an association that was to last for many years.

After Carl Schmedeman was completed and sailed from her Devonshire Dock berth I was sent back up to the top yard to work on the Orient liner Orsova. This ship was the last of the three mail liners built for the Orient Line in its post-war rebuilding programme. Although supposedly a sister ship to Orcades and Oronsay, she had many different and unusual features.

In his book *Origins, Orient and Oriana*, Orient Line chief naval architect Charles F Morris states Orsova was the first all-welded passenger liner to be built in Britain, and possibly the world. She was bigger and faster than her sister vessels and laid claim to being the world's first mastless liner.

The first all-welded pre-fabricated bottom units of Orsova were laid on number two berth early in 1952 and work on her went on at a good pace. As Orsova was being built, alongside her on number three berth was the partially completed aircraft carrier HMS Hermes. When work on her was stopped shortly after the end of the war the shell was up to the middle deck and the main internal bulkheads had been completed. For several years she lay in this state with the steel work being given regular coats of oil in an attempt to combat rust. When work began on her again, one factor in influencing this decision was that her berth was needed for passenger ships.

When the decision was made to recommence work on HMS Hermes it was found that there were only a few riveting squads left in the yard. Consequently, several squads of Scottish riveters were drafted in to complete the work.

Orsova and HMS Hermes grew side by side on adjacent berths and several of the shipwrights, myself included, were moved across to the warship to prepare for her launch. For a few days we lashed down anything that was liable to move or become dislodged during the launch.

On 16 February, 1953, we were aboard HMS Hermes when she was launched into Walney Channel by Lady Clementine, then Mrs Winston Churchill. I was positioned in a small compartment which was reached by descending about five vertical ladders. My job was to release one of the massive drag chain slips, and I had an apprentice with me to answer the temporary telephone and pass the release message on. Deep down inside the hull, in almost complete darkness and lit only by our hand-held torches, it was an eerie feeling awaiting the launch. A small chink of daylight came through the hole in the ship's side where the hinge of the slip passed through, but this did little to relieve the claustrophobic atmosphere.

As the apprentice and I sat there we could hear the creaking and groaning as thousands of tons of steel pressed down on the heavy wooden launch cradle, held back only by the triggers and yet striving to be free and moving.

Just seconds before the triggers were released and the ship began to move down the ways, my apprentice, who was on his first launch, decided he was suffering from claustrophobia and that he would feel better if he went into the fresh air. The danger of him climbing up several vertical ladders in the darkness of a strange ship was far greater than staying in his present position. As he made for the doorway and the ladder, I had to grab him and pull him back to hold him in a corner of the compartment. Barely had I done this when I heard the triggers drop and — after what appeared to be minutes but in reality was only seconds — HMS Hermes began her slide into her natural element. As the ship went down the ways and settled in the water I was able to calm the apprentice to the extent that he was able to carry out his duties at the telephone without any problems.

Once the drags were released and the ship was under tow we climbed up to the hangar deck to report to the foreman. On our way the apprentice thanked me for claming him down and allaying his fears. As I recall he also said that he would never go down on a launch again. And as far as I know, he never did.

Looking back now it seems rather ironic that Orsova, the all-welded ship that spelt out the end of the riveting era, was only to carry out her designated work for some twenty years whereas the riveted HMS Hermes is, in 1995, still afloat after a period of forty years.

It was not the method of construction that affected the longevity of either vessel but the purpose for which they were built. The development of the aeroplane, which was to prolong the life of the warship, was also the factor that sent Orsova and her sisters to a premature grave in the scrap yards during the early 1970s.

As Orsova was building it seemed that the airliner would not provide any serious competition to the passenger liners, particularly on the long route to Australia. But events occur throughout the world which, at the time, appear to be of no consequence to other industries.

In June 1819 the 320-ton Savannah became the first steamship to cross the Atlantic. Probably not much notice was taken of this event at the time but this new form of propulsion was to spell the beginning of the end for the sailing ship. It took approximately 100 years for the sailing ship to disappear completely from the oceans of the world, but the effect on the shipbuilding industry was felt much earlier.

As sail gave way to steam, wooden ships gave way to iron and steel, and builders of the wooden sailing vessels vanished from the rivers and shores of Britain. The most significant date for the 20th century builders of passenger liners was June 1969, exactly 150 years on from the time that

Savannah made her epic voyage. In that summer month an aircraft from the Boeing factory in Seattle arrived at the Paris Air Show. This aircraft, the 747, carried 442 passengers together with their baggage, mails and some cargo. From that fateful day the passenger liners were living on borrowed time.

But the end of the era was yet to come. I worked on Orsova assuming, as did all the shipbuilders of Barrow, that normally the life of a passenger liner was twenty to twenty-five years and that orders for other liners would always come in. How wrong we were.

On Orsova I worked with my mentor from apprentice days, shipwright Dennis Quayle, who ranked amongst the finest tradesmen in the yard. Dennis and I, working under foreman Bob Munro, fitted all the air-conditioning seats and machinery aboard the ship. Although the ship was not fully air-conditioned there was plenty to do and we worked in close conjunction with the contractors Thermotank Limited.

I was lucky enough to go on the sea trials of Orsova along with nine other shipwrights. After bottom cleaning in Gladstone Dock at Liverpool, Orsova recorded a speed of 26.08 knots over the measured mile on the Clyde. Work on her was not quite complete when we arrived in Tilbury and we stayed on her for a few more days before leaving for home. Three Vickers electricians sailed on her maiden voyage to Australia to complete some electrical work. During my trials period on Orsova I renewed several acquaintances with crew members from my Orcades days.

Once back home in the yard I worked on the outfit of tankers until I received an offer to join Orsova as assistant carpenter. There were Barrovians in legion serving in her crew. Second electrician Ken Pearson, plumber Fred Rawlings, deck storekeeper Jim Largue, chief butcher Alf Masson, third engineers Allan Jolley and Arthur Trelore, junior engineer Peter Hesketh and refrigerating engineer Eric Barton, are just some of the locally-born crew members who come to mind.

On one voyage to Australia we carried the England cricket team on the tour when under Len Hutton they won back the Ashes. During a practice session in nets rigged up on the tennis deck, Arthur Trelore completely frustrated the star English bowler Alec Bedser. He stopped every ball that Bedser bowled so much so that an article appeared in the ship's newspaper suggesting that Arthur be enlisted in the touring party as an opening batsman.

As passenger traffic to and from Australia was declining, Orsova spent some time cruising from Australia in addition to opening up new routes in the Pacific. On 22 February, 1955, Orsova broke a speed record for merchant ships which had stood for thirty years. She covered the 2,100 miles between San Francisco and Honolulu in three days and seventeen hours, nearly three hours less than the record time. My diary for that voyage records that we also broke the ship's speed record for one day's run, covering 585 miles in

24 hours. But records were of no use in the changing climate of passenger travel around the world. The fact had to be accepted that the passenger liner just could not compete with the airliner.

It was barely five years from the date that the 747 landed in Paris until the seas were all but cleared of passenger liners. By the end of 1975, Barrow-built liners such as Orcades, Oronsay, Orsova, Himalaya, Chusan, Presidente Peron, Eva Peron and Apapa, had all gone to a premature grave at the shipbreakers.

Little did the workers at the Barrow shipyard realise that after Orsova only one true passenger liner would be built in the yard. She, of course, was Oriana, of which more later, but even she was converted to a one-class cruise ship in 1973. Odessa, ex-Copenhagen, launched without ceremony on 20 December 1972, was designed as a cruise liner.

Following the sudden death of my father while I was home on leave, I left the Orient Line and once again joined the ranks of the Barrow shipbuilders.

The Orient Line Song

One Monday Morning the missus said now Bob
Go down to the Orient Line and get yourself a job
Now being a man of action I jumped aboard a tram
Twenty minutes later I was lavatory man

Chorus
Lavatory man, lavatory man
Twenty minutes later I was lavatory man

Oh the missus thinks I'm Purser
And she'd really have a fit . . .

. . . The rest is unprintable

74

Chapter 8

Dock Gates, Diversions and Destroyers

IN THE mid-1950s the Barrow shipyard was experiencing somewhat erratic periods of boom and slump. Construction of large tankers such as Spyros Niarchos and Evgenia Niarchos was in progress and the aircraft carrier HMS Majestic was nearing completion. But a world wide shortage of steel was holding up work in certain areas and the giant tankers were nowhere near as labour-intensive as the passenger liners had been.

One instance of this can be given by considering that accommodation on the liners was for around 1,500 passengers and crew. On a tanker the joiners would have to fit out the cabins for around 45 crew members only. Work for electricians and painters was also reduced as the tankers, with their cavernous empty cargo holds, needed next to no fitting out in these areas.

However, there was work for shipwrights.

When I applied for a job back in the yard at my trade, Mr Wilf Burns, the head foreman, followed his usual practice and kept me on the dole for about four weeks. As it turned out this was no real hardship as the Orient Line kept me on full pay until I had sorted out my domestic arrangements and resigned from their employment.

Once back in the yard I worked for a spell on HMS Melbourne, formerly HMS Majestic. Once she was commissioned into the Australian Navy there followed a period of work on a set of dock gates.

This work was on night shift right throughout the winter from January until Easter and working for five nights a week, 10pm until 7.30am. On the open dockside at Buccleuch Dock, this definitely was not the most pleasant of jobs.

The next move was on to HMS Hermes where I once again teamed up with shipwright John Rigg.

By early 1956, final plans for the aircraft carrier had been formulated and work was getting underway in earnest to complete the ship. Even the position of the steel bulkhead in the wardroom, which had been moved a reputed fifteen times, was finalised at last.

At one period it had been mooted by the shipwrights that this bulkhead be mounted on wheels to assist the seemingly endless movement of it around the decks. I understand that this bulkhead finished up within three inches of its original position.

John and I were working in the magazines of HMS Hermes fitting timber stowages for the ship's armament. We were paid sometimes on an average of the shipwrights piecework rate, which in reality was the rate that the head foreman thought appropriate. At other times our work would be assessed during the progress of the job and a piecework price fixed for each part of the operation.

While we were engaged in this magazine fitting out, new plans were received which meant an alteration to the work.

When the piecework counter, a staff member who also counted up the work of the caulkers, came to record the amount of work done, the alteration, which naturally entailed extra work, was pointed out to him and, as we thought, duly noted.

Our head foreman made the habit of visiting the dockside fitting out departments each afternoon and the afternoon following our count John and I were summoned before him. To our great surprise we were berated for being lazy, taking no interest in our work and not earning our pay. Apparently, the piecework counter had not mentioned the alteration to our job and despite all our protestations and explanations, and those of foreman Eric Kendall, Mr Burns refused to listen. This episode, which was to have repercussions beyond belief, took place on a Wednesday afternoon. Two days later, on the Friday morning, John and I were told to report to the foreman's office after our morning lunch break. When we arrived we were surprised to see the twenty or so shipwrights from the 'flying squad' also gathered in the adjacent store. Without ceremony, Mr Burns appeared from the office, shouted out our names, and told us we were all transferred to work at Cammell Laird's Liverpool shipyard.

Spelling out our conditions of employment he said: "Train fare paid to Liverpool, £10 a week wages with no overtime, £1 a week towards your lodgings. The work will be for an indefinite period. Any man refusing to go will be given his cards."

It was as if a bomb had gone off around us. None of us had any idea that such a transfer of labour was in the offing.

Someone asked why this action was being taken.

"Because of a shortage of steel," came back the reply.

It did not take long to figure out that John and I were the only two shipwrights included in this squad who were working on HMS Hermes. The fact that no other steelwork trades, such as platers or welders, were involved gave little substance to the shortage of steel story. When we added these facts to the reality that we were working on a woodwork job that would last for several months it became obvious that our comments to the head foreman two days previously had been instrumental in putting us in this predicament. Walking out of the store in a stunned condition, both John and I agreed that it was a bad deal and that we were not going to Liverpool.

Our average weekly wage on HMS Hermes was £11, and to receive the same amount and then pay lodgings from it was not by any means an attractive offer. John and I also had domestic reasons for not wanting to work in Liverpool for an indefinite period. When we saw Mr Burns on the Friday afternoon and told him of our decision his answer was brief and to the point.

"Get your cards then."

It is always said that next to the death of a loved one, divorce is the most traumatic experience in one's life. Any person, more so in this day and age, who has to go home and tell his wife he is out of a job will disagree with the latter part of the statement and substitute the word redundancy for divorce.

John and I, however, were not redundant. The word was in the dictionary but not in common use. Out of work was the term of the day, and redundancy money or redundancy pay were words of the future. We had been offered alternative work, so by our refusal to accept it we were deemed to have left the firm of our own accord. The Shipwrights Union, not amalgamated to the Boilermakers until some ten years later, could take no action or get the Liverpool rates increased.

The Barrow shipwrights who had been transferred to the Vickers Newcastle yard were on reasonable rates of pay and had a chance of overtime in addition to receiving a decent lodging allowance.

Work in the Barrow area was not really plentiful but both John and I had a stroke of luck. As we worked, not very hard I admit, in the magazine of HMS Hermes during our last week in the yard, we were still stunned by the recent developments and as all people in such situations do we kept asking ourselves: "Why us?" But it was no use brooding and by a hand of fate, or coincidence — call it what you will — Jack Jordan, the foreman for the Thermotank air-conditioning firm of contractors, came down into the magazine.

I had worked in close conjunction with the Thermotank company on Orsova, and when I asked Jack if he needed any men he immediately said: "If you will take a labourer's job you can start on Monday". Unfortunately, he could find no work for John but recommended him to Archie Glenn, the foreman of Newall Insulation Contractors. John and I finished in the yard on the Friday and commenced work with our new employers on the following Monday.

It was noticeable that during our last week in the yard our piecework counter did not arrive down the magazine to give us a count.

My job with Thermotank was to carry ventilation ducting aboard the ship and then assist the tradesman sheetmetal worker in its erection. Perhaps it was ironic that I worked on HMS Hermes erecting vent trunking in an area where I had worked as a shipwright.

John's job with the insulation contractors was to spray flock asbestos on to the bulkheads in the accommodation areas of the tankers fitting out. The dangers of asbestos had not been identified in those days and it was used for insulation on many buildings and projects. Although our wages as labourers were less than we earned as tradesmen, John and I had the chance to work some overtime which, in effect, more or less made up our money.

As regards the shipwrights who did go to work in Liverpool, within a few weeks most had returned either to go on the dole or to eventually take up new careers with firms such as the Electricity Board, Glaxo or Barrow Steelworks.

In the Autumn of 1956 the contingent of shipwrights who had been in Newcastle returned to the yard and investigations showed that there was a Shipwrights Wanted notice on the board in the Labour Exchange. Hearing this news, John and I stopped Mr Burns on the dockside one afternoon and asked him if he could start us back at our trade.

"Only if you are fit and strong," he said. "I've got too many cripples and sick men in the department as it is."

Upon receiving our assurances that we were in reasonable health he told us to report for work after giving a week's notice to our respective employers. John and I did not think his remark about cripples and sick men was in good taste, but it was typical of the attitudes adopted by persons in authority in those days. In fact, John, always the philosopher, remarked that sometimes words and feelings like that have a way of coming back on those who uttered them.

One consolation to John and I over our time spent away from the trade, and also to other shipwrights either working away or on the dole, was the fact that the union adhered to its principle that while there were local shipwrights out of work, no overtime would be worked in the yard. This edict was carried out to the letter.

Once we reported for work back at our trade, John and I were sent down to Devonshire Dock to work on the outfitting of HMS Eastbourne. She was one of a new class of frigates for the Royal Navy and had been towed down from her launching place on the Tyne for completion in Barrow. When we boarded her she was not much more than an empty hull.

I recall that we spent the first few days unshipping the loose bulkheads and part-welded structure from her in order to gain access to the machinery spaces. Our problem was a shortage of plans. None had been sent down from the Newcastle yard and none of her compartments had been identified and marked up accordingly.

Within a few days our immediate problem was solved. We obtained not only a general arrangement plan of this new class of frigate but also a sectional drawing giving details of all the ship's fitments, accommodation and weapons. One of our fellow shipwrights, I forget just who, brought in the centre page spread from his son's *Eagle* comic which was headed, "Britain's Latest Warship. Full Details of the New Frigates". Within a couple of weeks of putting this centre spread up in our store, some of the ship's petty officers, who had arrived to stand by her, had written to the publishers of *Eagle* and obtained copies of the drawing (photocopiers had not been invented in 1956).

No sooner had they been distributed to various trades than the peace of the dockside was shattered by the arrival of the local police, Vickers works guards and several big, hard looking characters wearing suits and ties. With the shipwrights' store being one of the first in line on the dockside the hit squad, for want of a better word, charged in and, as we heard later, enacted a scene similar to that of the TV series *Elliot Ness and the Untouchables* as they raided an illicit distillery. The words: "The building is surrounded, come out with your hands up," were not actually used, but the store door was crashed open and the order: "Stay where you are — Nobody leave the room," was given. This dramatic entrance by the law enforcement officers was something of a damp squib because the only person in the shipwrights' store was labourer Arthur Poole who was busy sweeping the floor. All the shipwrights were engaged docking an Isle of Man steamer in the graving dock.

Apparently the police, works guards and officers from the Special Branch, brought up from London, had made the raid in an effort to catch the culprits who were allegedly passing around secret plans of Britain's latest warship — the centre spread from the *Eagle*. The drawings were removed from all stores on the dockside but returned a couple of days later after it was confirmed that the artist's impression had been approved by the Admiralty who had supplied the information. We wondered at the time if the Russians placed orders for copies of the *Eagle.*

Under foreman Bob Munro, and with shipwright liners off Dave Crawford and Fred Halliday, John and I enjoyed our time on HMS Eastbourne. The ship's manager was Bill Richardson who in later years became managing director of the firm. It was on this ship that we first came across Big Cyril the welder, of whom more later.

One further memory of working on HMS Eastbourne was of fitting cringle, or hammock, bars in the crew mess decks. These bars had an indentation every 21in to which the centre holding rope of a hammock would be fastened. If there ever was an example of how the Royal Navy stuck to its traditions this was it. A hundred-and-fifty years after Nelson won the Battle of Trafalgar the seamen on Britain's latest warship were still allocated the same amount of sleeping space as their forebears on HMS Victory.

After HMS Eastbourne was completed John and I spent a period in the docking and repair squad. In this squad we docked Isle of Man Steam Packet vessels in the graving dock for their annual overhauls and also worked on the maintenance and repair of naval vessels of the Reserve Fleet. Eventually we were moved up to the top yard to work on the outfit of, and to prepare for the launch of, the Chilean destroyer Almirante Williams.

Over the years the Barrow shipyard built ships for many foreign navies and still well remembered are the destroyers built for some South American countries. The almost instant rapport that was established between the crews of these ships and the Barrovians made for happy working conditions aboard, and I have fond memories of working on both the Chilean destroyers Almirante Williams and Almirante Riveros.

Before the launch of the first ship, Almirante Williams, only a few senior officers were in town. On the launch day they were resplendent in their uniforms on the launch platform, accompanied by their ladies.

After the launch they waited by the dockside for the ship to moor up at her fitting out berth in Devonshire Dock. Foreman shipwright Bob Munro delegated John and myself to remove the remnants of the champagne bottle and its ribbon from the bow of the ship so that the ship's officers could keep them as souvenirs. We had barely secured the boat when two officers relieved us of the bottle and ribbon and gave us a £1 tip each. As John remarked after we had pocketed our tip: "If these Chileans are always as decent as this we are going to get on very well with them." And so we did.

A few months later some more of the crew arrived. They were sergeants, the Chilean equivalent of chief and petty officers. The sergeants had to take note of the work being done in their respective departments and to write a report about it. Some could speak good English and others were learning it reasonably well.

One engineering sergeant, who we later got to know quite well, would seek us out each day and ply us with questions about our current job.

One cold, wet, miserable day we were fitting some auxiliary seats in the engine room, and it must be said that with the rain dripping down our necks and the threat of an impending strike, John and I were not in the best of moods.

The sergeant, Diego by name, pestered us so much about our work that John, in the hopes that he would go away, told him that the machinery to be fitted later was a wigwam to wind the moon. Carefully and precisely Diego, with our help with the spelling, wrote this down in his little notebook, and apparently satisfied disappeared up the engine room ladder. A couple of days later all tradesmen working on the ship were told by their respective foremen that they were to cooperate fully with the ship's crew. In short, mickey taking and jokes about wigwams did not come under the heading of cooperation.

Big Cyril, the welder mentioned earlier, worked with us on these destroyers and he was, and still is, remembered as a character. Cyril didn't just speak. He shouted and bellowed to all and sundry at all times. His voice could be heard over the noise of half a dozen caulking hammers going at full strength, always grumbling about the job, the shipyard, the foremen and everyone around him, yet at the same time getting on with his job. Cyril was, to say the least, a character of repute.

When working on HMS Eastbourne, ship's manager Bill Richardson, always a quietly spoken gentleman, could do nothing but shake his head in despair when passing Cyril on the ship. Yet he always called for him when an awkward job cropped up.

The Chileans loved Cyril. In fact, they even took him out on trials with them. Not as a working member of the trials team but as a guest in their wardroom. When we fendered Almirante Williams out of Ramsden Dock for her first sea trials, Cyril was on the ship's bridge with the officer, pilot and ship's manager, hurling abuse at everyone within earshot. And that, with Cyril's voice range, included the whole of Barrow Island.

Our relationships with the Chileans grew. Many of the sergeants bought motorbikes and scooters and spent their spare time touring the local countryside. Sadly, our friend Diego was killed in an accident on Roose Bridge one Sunday morning when driving his scooter. Many of the workmen, including John and I, attended his funeral.

As Almirante Williams neared completion more of her crew arrived. These new arrivals were ordinary engine room crew, seamen and stewards and, to quote Cyril's rather uncouth expression: "Some of the beggars were straight out of the jungle." Perhaps this was exaggerating, but it must be said they had a lot to learn about ships.

During the sea boat's trials in the dock we witnessed the sight of the ship's whaler, or rowing boat, being rowed around the dock with the crew of Chilean seamen all facing towards the bow and the boat being rowed astern, much to the annoyance of the sergeant in the stern, trying to steer.

On another occasion the ship's manager, Harold Postlethwaite, observed a young crew member striking matches and peering into the oil fuel filling and sounding pipes occasionally dropping some of them, still lit, down the pipes. When tackled about this dangerous practice the offending seaman, in broken English, said: "It is OK. Matches are safety matches."

After this incident it seemed something of a relief when the gunnery department of the ship was supervised by British naval officers from Whale Island at Portsmouth, otherwise who knows where the shells would have landed when armament trials took place.

As Almirante Williams neared completion she underwent a series of sea and gunnery trials. It was during these latter trials that the trials party of workmen discovered that sea trials on a destroyer could turn out to be a hard way to earn a wage.

A few days before Christmas the ship went out for a supposedly 24-hour gunnery trial. At high water, around noon the following day, the ship was due back. It was blowing a force eight gale and after we had stood at Ramsden Dock for an hour, hardly able to stand up against the wind, we were told we would not be fendering her until the next tide at midnight. Conditions were apparently so bad that Almirante Williams had been forced to seek shelter in Ramsey Bay. The procedure was repeated on the evening tide. We stood in the pouring rain from 11.30pm till 12.30am when it was decided that the ship would definitely arrive on the midday tide. I recall that we were paid the bare two hours pay at bottom rate for this midnight call-out.

When the ship did arrive after 48 hours at sea and was fendered and tied up in the lock it was discovered that the trials party was far from happy. The ship had been provisioned for a 24-hour trial only, and for the 24 hours the ship had been at anchor in Ramsey Bay the only sustenance for the crew had been one bowl of tomato soup each. Adding to the discomfort of semi starvation and sea sickness was the fact that in those days most people were smokers and all aboard had exhausted their supply of cigarettes.

A couple of lorry drivers were sent immediately up the road to scour Barrow Island for hot pies and cakes and to return, also at high speed, with packets of cigarettes. Once these refreshments were passed on to the trials party, which included my mate John Rigg, things settled down somewhat and the ship eventually moored back at her berth in Devonshire Dock. However, all the workmen in the trials party were adamant that they would not go on sea trials again.

A couple of days later, when they received their Christmas pay, they found an extra £4 in their packets, courtesy of the Chilean Navy. Also included was a nicely-worded note apologising for the discomfort and inconvenience they had experienced on trials. It did not go unnoticed that the Chilean Navy had paid for both the hot pies and cigarettes as well as the extra money in their pay packets.

The firm, although responsible for the catering arrangements, made no comment. On further trials of the two Chilean destroyers, extra food was always carried and the former disgruntled trials party reversed their decision and had no further complaints about conditions.

The mention of trials brings to mind the story of a pair of pliers which nearly caused an international incident.

When Almirante Williams was fitting out, her three boats arrived from their makers at Southampton. As John and I were fitting the boat davits, we had to sign for the acceptance of the boats and their equipment. The equipment was taken off and booked into the outfit store at Buccleuch Dock while the boats were fitted and tested in their davits. The boats were then removed and not replaced until the ship went on trials. The equipment was also replaced in the boats. As the ship neared completion, all the equipment and stores allocated to the ship had to be handed over to the ship's crew and accepted by them before the ship could be signed over from her builders.

Our problem was that when John and I had signed for the boats and their equipment, we had accepted an inventory for the 16-foot motor boat, which included one tool kit for the engine. When the boats came up for inspection a full list of tools, required to be in the tool kit, was available to the sergeant boatswain.

This list was checked with the relevant tool kit and everything was accounted for except one pair of pliers. For a few days the sergeant hounded John and I for the missing pliers. We had signed for a tool kit and had no knowledge of whether the pliers had been in the kit or had got lost or stolen on trials.

Eventually the story of the pliers reached through to high places and we had to explain the situation to the ship's manager. The Chilean Navy was refusing to accept the ship from the builders unless they had the missing pair of pliers. Several meetings were held between the ship's officers and Mr Postlethwaite, and an ultimatum was given that the pliers had to be supplied within two days.

As the situation appeared to be getting out of hand, Mr Postlethwaite sent for foreman shipwright Bob Munro, and handing him a £1 note told him to acquire some pliers before war broke out. Bob Munro passed the money to labourer Arthur Poole with orders to acquire some pliers poste haste. Within half an hour the pliers incident was over and honour satisfied on both sides.

Arthur had purchased a pair of pliers from an apprentice electrician at the Sub Dock for, I believe, ten shillings (50p). And as the Bard says: "All's well that ends well". The Chileans got their pliers, John and I were exonerated and off the hook, the apprentice electrician was happy — as was the labourer who was ten bob better off.

Probably even Mr Postlethwaite was happy. He was £1 out of pocket but he got the ship handed over to the Chilean Navy without any further problems.

Other incidents stick in my mind from those days working on Chilean destroyers.

The Chilean sergeants standing by their ship had their offices underneath and adjacent to the 250-ton crane at Devonshire Dock, near to the ship's gangway. On the day we ceased work for our Christmas holidays they stood outside their offices, giving all the workmen going aboard a bottle of beer each and a packet of twenty cigarettes. This gesture was much appreciated by the workforce and did a lot to further good relations between workmen and crew.

Before the ship left Barrow it was decided that all the goods bought locally by the crew, motor cycles, scooters, washing machines, radios, etc, could be transported to Chile stowed aboard the ship. John and I had the job of getting additional openings burned on the ship in order to stow all these bulky items down in the two crew messes at the aft end. Apparently, such luxury goods were either in short supply in South America or the rate of exchange was such that it was more profitable to buy them in England.

Other stories could be told of work on the Chilean destroyers and of the activities of their crews, particularly with regard to the young ladies in the area. But space dictates we move on.

Shortly before each destroyer left Barrow for the last time, a party to end all parties was held in the Duke of Edinburgh hotel, and I understand that the guest of honour was Big Cyril who sang many unprintable songs before he collapsed under the table.

I still treasure a silken pennant which was presented to me and others who worked on these happy Chilean warships all those years ago.

At the time of writing it is reported that the Almirante Williams and Almirante Riveros are still afloat and in commission.

— Chapter 9 —

From Outfit and Oriana to Loftsman

AS ALMIRANTE Riveros neared completion, John Rigg and I were moved across to Buccleuch Dock to work on the final stages on the outfitting of Oriana, the largest liner ever to be built in Barrow.

John was given the job of planing and finishing the wood decks while I was engaged in fitting lifeboat chocks and general outfit work.

During the couple of months I worked on Oriana I renewed old friendships with her crew, many of whom were old shipmates from my Orcades and Orsova days.

One incident worthy of mention occurred during the latter stages of Oriana's fitting out. Many people who worked on her may recall the day that she took on a severe list to port while afloat in Buccleuch Dock. Involved in the incident was shipyard fitter Fred Scott, one of the nicest characters you could wish to meet. Fred started his time as an apprentice fitter in 1937 and during the war worked long hours on the many ships that came into Barrow docks for urgent repair work. Fred worked on most of the post-war passenger liners that were built in the yard and went on the sea trials of more than thirty ships, ranging from liners to tankers.

When working on the Oriana he was sent with another fitter to service a valve in the propeller shaft tunnel. They were told to wait for the foreman before starting work. As Fred walked into shaft tunnel, well below the waterline, a spout of water hit him and his mate and nearly washed them off their feet. Another fitter had been given the job before Fred and had failed to take certain elementary precautions before stripping the top cover off the sea inlet valve.

As the water of Buccleuch Dock poured into the shaft passage, Fred and his mate, helped by shipwrights John Rigg and Horace Killip, worked up to their waists in water and eventually, after a hard struggle, managed to fit a temporary blanking cover over the valve. This action stemmed the flow of water enough to enable a diver to put a temporary patch on the outside of the hull and for the fire brigade to pump out the water.

As many tradesmen worked at their jobs on the Oriana few were aware of the drama that was taking place far below them in the shaft tunnel.

Although Oriana took a severe list to port during this incident, no damage was done.

Fred and his mate were taken home in a fire brigade mini-bus and told that they would be paid for the remainder of the working day. John told me later it was around 4pm when he got home so he obtained only one hour's pay for his efforts. He and the other men who saved Oriana from sinking were thanked for their efforts but were given no compensation towards the cleaning or replacement of their clothes and footwear.

Fred Scott also played for Barrow Rugby League and reckoned he was the only player to be sent off at Craven Park to a standing ovation. He was fond of telling the story of how, when playing against Liverpool Stanley in front of a crowd of 10,000, one of the opposing players roughed up several of the Barrow team. When he started to give Fred a hard time he retaliated and, to quote Fred: "He did not get up for a while, but I had made my point and before the referee could send me off I walked away and off the field to a standing ovation from the crowd."

Fred Scott was just one of the many Barrovian characters who were a pleasure to work with and also a fine example of the skilled tradesmen who helped build the ships for which Barrow is famous.

When Oriana passed through the entrance gates of Ramsden Dock on 4 November, 1960, and out into Walney Channel to begin her sea trials, little did the thousands of onlookers who waved her goodbye realise they were witnessing the end of an era. Oriana was the last of the true passenger liners to be built at Barrow. She was the last ship ever to wear the distinctive Orient Line livery of a corn-coloured hull, because in 1965 the P&O company acquired the outstanding minority shares in the Orient Line and painted her white to conform with the other ships of the P&O.

In May 1986 Oriana left Sydney Australia, under tow, to become a floating hotel at Oita near Bappu, the hot spring resort on the island of Kyushu, Japan. At the time of writing, Oriana, the last of the liners, is still afloat in her new role. But it is perhaps better to recall Oriana as the stately passenger ship that represented the biggest and best of the Barrow-built liners.

After Oriana left Barrow I went back to working mates with John Rigg on Britain's first nuclear submarine, HMS Dreadnought, which was launched on Trafalgar Day, 1960. Not much outfitting had been done on Dreadnought before her launch, and she was very much an empty hull when John and I went to work on her.

It was on Dreadnought that I first came into contact with the then new process of arc-air gouging. This process is, to put it simply, a reversal of electric welding — where the electric welder uses a rod of steel to join or build up metal. The arc air gouger uses a copper-coated carbon rod to melt steel away. Gouging is used mainly to cut away and shape the steelwork, preparatory to welding submarine units or heavy castings together.

When the gouger has finished his work the gouged area is then cleaned up by a tradesman using a hy-cycle grinder. This is a hand-held electric grinding machine that can cut through, or buff, and shape metal at high speed. The fumes given off from the gouging process are noxious, choking and dense, to the extent that within seconds of the gouger starting work a compartment can be filled with a thick, lung-burning fog.

There can be no disputing that the arc-air gouger has the dirtiest, unhealthiest and most uncomfortable job in the shipbuilding industry. Before gouging work commences the metal adjacent to the area to be worked has to be preheated to a temperature of around 121 degrees or over. This is done by the plant electricians fitting electric elements covered in asbestos to the surrounding metal to bring it to the working temperature. With an intermittent spluttering, whooshing hiss, the metal is melted and blown away in a cascade of gleaming white-hot sparks by the compressed-air emitted from the mouth of the gouging tongs.

When gouging was first introduced the firm installed no extra ventilation in the vicinity of the work and stated that the fumes and subsequent fog given off by the process were not a hazard to health. It will not be hard for the layman to understand that in the long steel pipe that comprises the hull of a submarine, there will not be many openings for men or ventilation. Consequently, men working in the area where gouging was taking place were subject to all the hazards and discomforts that were associated with the gouging work. The same can be said of those who worked near the welders and grinders.

Even the hy-cycle grinder added his share of fumes and dirt to the ships under construction. The harsh sibilant screech of metal being torn away to form a shower of red-hot carbon sparks signalled that the hy-cycle grinder was adding his share to the task of building a ship. He too had to wear a protective hood, mouth and nose mask and face mask to carry out his arduous task. Over the years, showers and washing facilities have been provided for the gougers, but only because of pressure from the unions and eventual realisation that the gouger has the dirtiest job in shipbuilding.

Perhaps this rather lengthy explanation of the work of the gougers and grinders will help the reader to understand something of the conditions that prevail in the shipbuilding industry, and also some of the reasons why the workforce and their unions are so insistent about the upholding of health and safety regulations.

My memories of work on Dreadnought are still of the fumes that pervaded the vessel with the introduction of gouging, but upon further reflection it must be said that at the time no one realised the amount of ventilation that was required when this arc-air gouging process was fully underway.

It was when I worked on Dreadnought during the early part of 1961 that all the shipwrights in the yard were paid off because of a ban on overtime working. This dispute was due to the firm's insistence that a shift work system be implemented without — the shipwrights thought — due consultation and agreement on compensatory pay for working on shift work.

After the short-lived dispute was over I worked on Dreadnought again for a few weeks then was moved back to the Chilean destroyer Almirante Riveros, which was nearing completion.

For the next month or so I began to feel like a gipsy or New Age traveller, never staying on one job for more than a few weeks at a time. Head foreman Wilf Burns had died and his position was taken by foreman shipwright John Preece. Mr Preece decided it would be a good policy to move some of his men away from their normal jobs to give them more experience. At least that was his story.

My first job when moved from the destroyer was in the new assembly shop at the top yard where I worked on piecework on the refitting and refurbishing of the lock gates from Ramsden Dock. This job lasted for about three weeks and consisted of cleaning up and refacing the greenheart timber from the dock gate sill. As regards the story of my alleged chasing of the piecework assessor the full length of the assembly shop while waving my adze at him, I offer no comment except to say I was soon moved from this job to spend a few weeks in the launchway squad. Work in the launchway squad was on a contract basis and not piecework.

The next job was to go back to the traditional shipwright's work of caulking. But not by any means the caulking of a ship's deck. I went to work with veteran shipwright Teddy Banks and our job was to caulk the floor of the grandstand at Holker Street football ground, the home of Barrow AFC. Apparently, during the previous season a fire had started in the dressing rooms and offices below the stand, and the cause was alleged to have been through cigarette ends falling through the gaps in the plank flooring. To prevent a re-occurrence of this incident it was decided that caulking the gaps in the floor would be appropriate. Each day Teddy and myself were transported on the back of a lorry from the yard to the football ground where we worked under the supervision of foreman Charlie Harmon, a keen soccer supporter. A labourer also accompanied us to boil up the pitch which was put into the deck — or should I say floor — seams after the oakum or tarry rope was hammered in. Each morning before we arrived at the football ground we had a mystery tour around the town calling at various houses to unload large bags of firewood, supposedly destined for our pitch boiler.

The work at Holker Street was not unduly hard as we did not have to complete a full berth — 125 feet — of caulking each day. I recall that the football season had not yet begun and the weather was pleasantly fine. We were also able to watch the soccer team engaged in pre-season training under manager Ron Staniforth. When the job was completed we were thanked for our services by Mr Staniforth and given a bottle of beer each along with a ground season ticket for the forthcoming season. I must confess that being a lifelong supporter of the Barrow rugby league team I gave the ticket away, but I enjoyed the beer.

The Holker Street grandstand has been recently demolished to make way for a new and safer structure. At least I can say that with the many jobs I worked on during this period in the shipyard, caulking a grandstand at a football ground has to be classed as rather different for the normal shipwright's work.

After the Holker Street job I was back on the road again and the next job was working in the submarine mock-up shop at the top yard. This work entailed making a full-size replica of the submarine in wood and was very much an ongoing labour-intensive job which involved many shipwrights. Before I could enter the mock-up shop I had to be screened and obtain a pass from the security department. Despite the fact that I had worked on the real submarine and had been screened for that sort of work, I had to stand outside the mock-up shop until my security pass and clearance was approved.

A few weeks later I was on the move again. The next job was working on the nightshift in the new assembly shop where I was engaged on ironwork on the construction of submarine units. During this period the nightshift hours consisted of working four nights a week and then a Friday afternoon shift from 4.30pm until 8pm. After a few weeks on nights in the assembly shop I was on the move yet again.

Head foreman John Preece came in early one morning and called me out from a submarine unit saying: "I've got a new job for you. Come with me and I'll introduce you to your new head foreman in the mould loft."

After sixteen years as a shipwright in the yard, the only thing I knew about the mould loft was its location above the West Shop. As we walked through the yard I was told that I had been selected to become a loftsman and that I had better get used to the idea whether I liked it or not. I suppose this could be called being made an offer you daren't refuse.

Author Michael Dick, in his book *The 4.15 for Cartsdyke, A Tale of Two Shipyards, Scotts and the Greenock Dockyard,* wrote: "The shipwright is involved in every stage of building ships from the beginning of the gestation period through to the end of the trials."

Going up the many steps to the mould loft on a September morning in 1961 I realised that I had worked on all stages of shipbuilding, except for the gestation period, and this was about to commence.

FENDERING at Ramsden Dock. The Chilean destroyer Almirante Williams leaves for sea trials, and the shipwright in the foreground may take his hands out of his pockets and pick up the plank fender at his feet, just in case the ship does look like touching the dock wall (photo North West Evening Mail)

TRADITIONAL hand-caulking the wood deck on Oriana. The shipwrights in this case are using cotton instead of oakum (tarry rope) for driving into the seams (photo VSEL)

THE deck seams are payed (filled) with hot pitch (photo VSEL)

JOHNNIE Black (third from left) receives a "golden loft nail" (made in the works) and a silver tea service from veteran loftsman John Crossfield, upon his retirement after fifty years as a loftsman. Left to right: Jimmy Kitley, Bill Allington, Johnnie Black, Fred Swindlehurst, John Crossfield, Bill Gradwell (photo VSEL)

BUILDING the lower forward end of the cruise liner Copenhagen (later Odessa) in the new assembly shop (photo North West Evening Mail)

Chapter 10

Piecework to Loftwork — Life in the Loft

THE Barrow shipyard mould loft was situated in a loft or an attic above the West Shop and it was a place where complex moulds, patterns, shapes, templates, mock-ups and models were developed and constructed by loftsmen and mould makers.

The whole building was built as a shell shop during World War One by the Combustion Works of Derby. The loft itself runs the full length of the West Shop. It is approximately 300ft long and 100ft wide. In 1961, with its poor lighting — both natural and artificial — its leaky roof and lack of adequate heating, it was much the same as when it was originally built. The black painted floor on which we worked was basically a large blackboard on which the full-size shape of a ship was drawn in chalk.

The provisional shape was drawn in from figures and information supplied by the ship drawing office and naval architects department. This shape, or lines, were then transferred into different views: plans, body and sections, with the loftsman fairing the lines in the different views. This fairing was done by means of long wooden battens nailed temporarily to the floor until all the lines gave a fair shape without any bumps or hollows. Once this was done, and the figures were approved by the drawing office, further lines were chalked in on the loft floor to determine the positions, measurements and shapes of frames. Thousands more measurements were then lifted or taken from the loft floor and entered into an offset book. From this offset book, which gave all the information appertaining to the shape of the ship's hull, the sections through the ship were drawn onto plywood boards and then scrieved or cut into the timber to form a permanent full-size record of the shape. From these boards, any shape throughout the ship could be determined. The loftsmen would then develop, expand and define the shape and size of the ship's plates and turn this information into templates for the plater to work the steel.

It was into this environment I was thrust and where I was to work for the next eleven years.

The loft department itself consisted of about sixty men who worked as loftsmen, mould makers, liners-off and mock-up shipwrights in various parts of the yard under head foreman Gilbert (Gib) Darragh. Mr Darragh was a large imposing figure and, it must be said, something of a gentleman and traditionalist of the old school of shipbuilders. His motto appeared to be that if an idea or method had not been adopted and used before, it was not going to be applied now.

To mention a couple of examples. One part of the loftman's work consisted of drawing out on hardboard the exact shape of steelwork such as rudder and hydroplane forgings and castings from which the patternmaker, iron founder and machinist would produce the finished article. Despite many suggestions that the hardboard be painted white to enable the lines and figures to be seen more clearly, Mr Darragh opposed this idea on the grounds of cost. Anyone who has put pencil marks on hardboard and tried to work to them in a poor light, such as was prevalent in the platers shop and mould loft, will be aware of the difficulties encountered.

Many apprentices, shipwrights, platers and draughtsmen spent part of their training in the mould loft. During my apprenticeship we never got the chance.

Mr Darragh would, again in an attempt to cut costs, ceremoniously cut pencils in half before issuing them to apprentices, on the theory they were not likely to do as much work as the tradesmen. There was just no answer to that line of thinking. It was just his way and was accepted as such, but he treated his men with respect and in return got the respect of his men.

One other habit he had was of walking in a straight line wherever possible across the loft floor. If you had a series of lines drawn on the floor or were in the process of lifting a tracing of lines and it was in the head foreman's path — it was just too bad. Consequently, it was not uncommon to see the imprints of his size ten shoes all over your job. On occasions you even had to move quickly to avoid your hands being trodden on. Everyone else who came into the mould loft followed the unwritten law of walking clear of jobs on the floor.

The foreman in the mould loft was Johnnie Black, who to many people — myself included — was the most unforgettable man you could ever meet. If George Best, Ian Botham, and Mohammed Ali were born to be the top of their professions then John Black was born to be the finest loftsman and shipbuilder ever to work in the Barrow yard.

He came to Barrow early this century when his father brought his family from Scotland to become the first pipe major of Barrow's St Andrews Pipe Band. For fifty years Johnnie worked on the mould loft floor at Vickers, drawing the complex lines and shapes of every type of vessel, and was a mentor and friend to all who knew him.

Many apprentice ship draughtsmen and apprentice shipwrights spent part of their training in the mould loft, and Johnnie Black always spoke highly of Len, later Sir Leonard, Redshaw, who as an apprentice ship draughtsman worked with him for a time.

He also had fond memories of Bill Richardson who started his apprenticeship as a shipwright. It was while he worked with Johnnie Black in the mould loft that his ability was noted and Johnnie put his reputation on the line when he persuaded the chief draughtsman to take Bill Richardson into the drawing office along with another two apprentices. At the time, such a transfer of apprentices was unheard of, but over the years Johnnie's faith in the lads was vindicated as they all rose to positions of authority with Bill Richardson eventually becoming managing director of the firm.

During the war, when Johnnie was just a shop floor loftsman, he was a specialist on the construction and development of such complex structures as propeller bossings, rudders and stern frames, many of which were cast and forged in foundries all over the country. Between working on the loft floor he had to travel by train and bus to factories throughout Britain to check, approve and accept the quality and accuracy of these castings. The conditions which existed in the wartime years made travelling difficult and Johnnie had to contend with air raids, train disruptions and delays. Only an ordinary workman, he received no extra money for these journeys and was permitted to stay in only the cheapest boarding houses. Now teams of staff do exactly the same job with far better conditions and allowances.

On one occasion a destroyer was being repaired in Barrow after her stern was blown off by a mine. Johnnie's expertise helped her get back to sea in record time. He recalled the location of some rejected propeller castings, ordered them to be delivered to Barrow, then modified them to suit, thus avoiding a long delay or the possible scrapping of the ship.

Johnnie Black was by far the most likeable and knowledgeable man I have ever met. He could motivate his men, teach them the complicated trade of a loftsman, spot a mistake or error in a moment, tell a fund of stories and never have a wrong or bad word to say about anyone. Yet he became a foreman only by accident.

In his fifties, and disgruntled by the low money and poor conditions in the yard at the time, he accepted a job in a shipyard at Hull. On the day he was due to leave, Len Redshaw, then the top man in the yard, heard by chance of his pending departure. Within thirty minutes Johnnie was summoned to his office and made an offer he couldn't refuse. He became foreman of the mould loft.

One story Johnnie used to tell about himself was of the Sunday morning he was gardening at his house in Black Butts Lane, on Walney Island, and head foreman Gib Darragh arrived.

"You have got to go to Liverpool immediately," he said to Johnnie. "One of the liners on trials is in dock with the anchor stuck in the hawse pipe. Mr

Redshaw is waiting in the company car at your gate to take you now to solve the problem."

Johnnie, not bothered in the slightest by the presence of the great Len Redshaw, whose word was comparable to a command from the Almighty, calmly replied: "Tell him I can't go today, I've promised to take my daughter up the park after dinner to feed the ducks."

Johnnie went to Liverpool the next day and solved the problem. Perhaps it was this unflappability that enhanced Len Redshaw's respect for him.

During my first few weeks of working in the loft I realised I was watching the actual birth of a ship as the lines were faired and the building offsets taken and recorded. The work, particularly when you spent hour after hour on your knees or haunches, crawling around the loft floor during the laying off of lines and lifting of offsets, was hard but interesting. I also had to delve deep into my memory to recall the basics of trigonometry and geometry in order to compete with the young apprentices who were learning such aspects of the loftsman's trade at day and night school. However, the ubiquitous Johnnie Black was always at had to help anyone who was having difficulty with the development of shapes such as square to round or offset cones.

Life in the loft was, apart from being more interesting than life as a shipwright, more comfortable. No longer did I have to work out in the rain, wind or snow and be dependent on the welders or burners whose whims, or inclination to work under the piecework system, determined the amount of money in my pay packet. An added bonus was the fact that the wage was constant with an additional eleven shillings (55p) a week being paid above the shipwrights average piecework rate.

During the early and mid-1960s, the firm was keen on bringing apprentices into shipbuilding and many schools were encouraged to take their older pupils on a tour of the shipyard. When such a tour was forthcoming, Gib Darragh would warn us beforehand to be on our best behaviour and to answer any questions that may be put to us by the schoolchildren or the teachers. When the party arrived, Gib would meet them at the door to personally give them the grand tour of the mould loft. Certain items, such as big templates, wooden mockings which the plater shaped his plates to, and models of the forward end of ships with their model anchors installed, would be arranged around the loft floor.

Once Mr Darragh got into his stride there was no stopping him with his commentary on all the technical terms appertaining to shipbuilding and loft work. Words such as buttock lines, water lines, body views, sheer, camber, half breadths and diagonals would be used much the same as a double glazing salesman of today would give his spiel and baffle the uninitiated with science.

One of his favourites was parabolic curve, which he used, incorrectly, to describe a ship's camber, and it came into the lecture as often as possible.

At the end of each tour the head foreman, having thoroughly confused his captive audience, would then ask if there were any questions. I recall such a day in the middle of winter when the rain was coming down in torrents, attempting an imitation of Niagara Falls. He concluded his grand tour and then asked for questions. One young lad, seemingly interested in what he had seen, said: "Please sir, what are all the buckets and empty cans spread around the floor for?"

An embarrassed and crestfallen head foreman could only say: "To catch the rain as it comes through the roof."

Needless to say, no further questions were asked and all the loftsmen within earshot were doubled up with laughter.

The working dress of the older loftsmen was a khaki warehouse coat, but between the wars I understand they came to work in a suit and sported a collar and tie to enhance their believed status of being a class above the ordinary workman.

Johnnie Black used to tell of one loftsman who stood out above the rest by virtue of always being very smartly dressed. Apparently, his wife worked as a cleaner for a local doctor and was always given the doctor's old suits for her husband to wear. Whenever the loftsman came to work looking extra smart he was given the dirtiest jobs to do. On the day he retired he asked the head foreman if there was anything personal about him being given all the dirty jobs. The head foreman, after giving him his retirement gift and praising his ability and timekeeping, said: "No, there was nothing personal it was just that you were better dressed than me and I didn't like that because it lowered my status as head foreman."

Johnnie Black and Gib Darragh were keen, no avid, no fanatical, supporters of Barrow AFC. If we were working overtime on Saturday afternoon during the football season the two men would come round the loft floor, check that everyone had enough work to carry on with, then at 2.30pm prompt, vanish through the door on their way to Holker Street football ground. Although left unsupervised, we never took any undue advantage of the fact but carried on with our jobs as normal. On the following Monday morning the head foreman and foreman would emerge from the office a few minutes after starting time to enact an action replay of Saturday's match for anyone who would listen. Once these graphic descriptions and demonstrations of how Fred Else saved a penalty or of how McEvoy tackled a centre forward were over it was back to work.

Many people will have experience of how, when you go to work in a small squad or office, it takes a while to be accepted by the old timers who often show resentment against newcomers to the department. The mould loft was a typical example of this clannish, small-town, don't want newcomers attitude. The older men had served their apprenticeship in the department and did not readily accept the intrusion of younger shipwrights who might, in their estimation, eventually take over their jobs. However, after a year or two, you did get accepted as a member of the department — by most loftsmen anyway.

During the eleven years I worked on the loft floor, one of the older tradesmen thought my name was There. If we passed each other on the shop floor I would greet him with: "Good morning George." I would get the answer: "Hello There." On the few occasions we had to work together I assume someone told him my name was Alan and he addressed me as such at the time. The following day I was back to being called There.

Loftsmen worked in close liaison with the West Shop platers or plater marker-offs who worked in the shop below the loft. We made battens and templates and supplied information to them for marking, cutting, rolling and shaping the ship's plates which would later be put together in the assembly shop.

Names such as Jimmy Batty, Jack and Jimmy Thompson, Jack Hornby, Jimmy Kitley, Shabber Dawson and Les Burns come to mind as being top tradesmen. Very often the same men could help us with our work by quoting an easier or alternative way to do the job which would also be to their advantage.

When Johnnie Black did his rounds of the men on the loft floor he would first check on your work, help you if you were having problems, then always find time to have a chat, often about anything under the sun.

Johnnie always had a fund of stories to tell about people, and the tale of Little Billy must rank as one of his best. A few years before, most departments in the yard had one man who was able to get all the bits of gear that were needed for the progress of the job and also the home projects for his workmates. In short, he was a handyman and Little Billy was definitely a king among handymen. Billy was a man who could get things done and knew everything worth knowing. He knew where every job was made and could chart its progress to the appropriate department. He knew the latest cricket score, who had been picked for the England soccer team, and not only the winner of the 3.30 race but also the second and third and their starting prices. Billy was also the shop steward and the general Mr Fixit for the department.

His domain was in a reasonably free and easy department where everyone worked together and the jobs got done efficiently and on time. His various services were appreciated by the workmen, some of which ranged from mending punctures on their bikes to acquiring several gallons of white emulsion paint and even supplying the coffee jars to take it home in. The head foreman chose to ignore Billy but was well aware of his activities.

In fact, the head foreman ignored most of his workforce except when issuing directives from the office, which made him unpopular and, indeed, hated by some. Part of the problem was that the head foreman worked religiously to the book. It was even said that if he got a note from the management stating that he had to jump into Walney Channel at 10am on Friday his only query would be from which slipway should he jump.

A few months before the head foreman was due to retire, the firm decided to have a purge, pogrom, crackdown, or best use of the working day as it would be called today. To interpret this directive the head foreman decided that Billy would have to curtail his activities. The department was in a state of shock. Billy was not very happy and less so when he was prevented from running his normal sweep on the Derby. In fact, he was adamant when the foreman asked him to arrange the collection and presentation for the head foreman's retirement that no one in the department would contribute anything towards a present, as all would be glad to see him go.

However, the foreman was obviously something of a diplomat and said to Billy: "You turn up with the present on the day and I'll try to calm things down with the Evil One." He was using one of the more polite expressions for the head foreman. Billy reluctantly accepted this chore and kept something of a low profile, but he did start selling cigarettes to his workmates, pushing a certain brand in particular.

The great day arrived when the Evil One was due to retire. Billy arrived at work with his holdall bulging and questions about the retirement present came thick and fast, but Billy would only say: "Wait and see." Ten minutes before the head foreman was due to return from lunch, Billy revealed his master stroke. He brought out a gleaming stainless steel coffee set complete with milk jug, sugar basin and tray saying: "This is it. This is the retirement present to which you have all contributed."

The ceremony went off like clockwork. The shop foreman made the presentation. The head foreman made a speech and the workmen clapped, albeit half-heartedly, and the men returned to their jobs. It was not until later in the afternoon when the head foreman had taken tea and biscuits with the management and Billy returned with the winner of the 3.30 that the secret of the presentation was revealed.

"I knew no one would donate any money towards the presentation so I saved all the coupons from the cigarettes I sold you and sent them off to get the coffee set," he said.

After receiving the congratulations for his efforts from both the shop foreman and his workmates, Billy drew himself up to his full 5ft 2in and said: "I didn't mind. Actually, it was quite a worthwhile exercise because the cigarettes were from the Coop and my wife collected the divi (dividend) on the money."

The location of the workshop where this incident took place was not revealed by Johnnie Black because somewhere in Barrow is a gleaming stainless steel coffee set which is assumed to have been donated by the voluntary contributions of a loyal workforce. Or so the inscription reads — but who do you think got it engraved and where? As Johnnie Black said: "Billy was truly a king among handymen."

It was during my early years in the mould loft that I first came into close contact with Leonard Redshaw. I was given the job of making a one inch to the foot model of the forward end of the methane tanker Methane Princess. This was always done to prove that the anchors would house correctly in the ship's hawse pipes. A scale model wooden anchor complete with a length of wooden chain was produced for the job by the older shipwrights who worked in the gun mock-up shop which was part of the department. As I was cutting out the shape of the frames on the bandsaw Johnnie Black said: "The angle of the hawse pipe is wrong, the plan will have to be altered, so cut out the timber for two models but only assemble one."

When the first model was made and the anchor tried in it, Johnnie was proved correct. The anchor just would not house in the pipe. Jobs such as this had to be approved or altered by the drawing office so the appropriate draughtsman was sent for. The section leader draughtsman, along with the draughtsman who had drawn the plan and supplied the provisional figures, arrived.

With them came the ship's manager, a gentleman who had earned for himself the nickname of Sackem Smith. Mr Smith had, at the time, just made his latest gaffe by sacking three burners for drinking tea. The three men had their punishment reduced to two weeks suspension. This reduction in sentence was due to the fact that they were the three top burners on the ship and no others were deemed suitable for the highly skilled job of burning in the shell plating butts. Consequently, construction work on the ship was held up and Sackem Smith was reputed to have been a bit too enthusiastic with his punishment.

However, my model of the forward end was inspected, the figures checked from the plan, and the anchor tried out. But still it would not stow and house correctly in the hawse pipe. The senior draughtsman, backed up by Mr Smith, tried to convince Johnnie Black that an alteration of a couple of degrees to the angle of the hawse pipe would solve the problem. Johnnie would not agree. He said that an alteration of at least ten degrees was necessary and that a new model should be made to prove it. The junior draughtsman said nothing, and I didn't know enough about the job to say anything.

The situation was getting out of hand with Sackem becoming more and more vociferous, belligerent and aggressive towards Johnnie when, like a genie appearing from Aladdin's lamp, Leonard Redshaw arrived on the scene accompanied by Bill Richardson. It was as if the cavalry had arrived at the last minute before the first shots of war were fired.

"Good morning Johnnie," said the great man. "Are you having problems?"

By this time I was very much on the outskirts of the job as Johnnie explained the situation and demonstrated the non-housing of the anchor on the model.

"What's the solution then?" said Mr Redshaw to Johnnie, after hearing the view of the draughtsmen and Mr Smith.

"Make a new model and alter the angle twelve degrees, that should do it."

Diplomatically addressing the others involved, Mr Redshaw effectively closed the subject by saying: "I think Mr Black has the experience to get the job right, so I suggest that we adopt his ideas and let him get on with it."

With that, he and Mr Richardson walked away leaving the section leader draughtsman, Sackem and the draughtsman, offering to return in a week's time to see the new model.

This was probably one of the few occasions in the shipyard where the knowledge of an experienced practical man triumphed over the theories of the technical man. It must be admitted that the appearance of Mr Redshaw, who was on one of his unannounced occasional tours around the yard, certainly played some part in solving the problem. Within a couple of days I had constructed a new model from the timber cut out earlier and altered the angle of the hawse pipe by Johnnie's required twelve degrees. The anchor then came up perfectly in all positions and the figures were approved without comment a week later.

The above story indicates not only something of Johnnie Black's skills but also the fact that Len Redshaw, having worked on the shop floor as an apprentice, knew his men well and had faith in their abilities.

During the fitting out of Methane Princess I had to go aboard to design and make a small alteration to the run of the anchor chain on the deck. This was fitted by shipwrights Teddy Rudd and Norman Wooff with their apprentice Jimmy Dunn, and the anchor trials went off perfectly. Tom Blacklock was then the manager on Methane Princess, Sackem Smith having departed for pastures new. After anchor trials, Mr Blacklock sent for me and my apprentice Norman Wright and thanked us for our work. Praise and thanks from a manager in those days was very rare and probably appreciated all the more. The credit, though, should obviously have gone to the man with the experience and know-how, Johnnie Black.

In the mid-1960s, Gib Darragh took ill and was off work for several weeks leaving Johnnie Black in charge of the department. Work proceeded as normal except that full-size pencils were issued when required and the hardboard sheets were painted white, which made life a lot easier for all.

Above the benches at one end of the loft about twenty-five builder's half-models of ships were secured to the wall. These half-models were works of art. Made up of layers of yellow pine, every plate on the hull and thickness and position was marked as an aid to draughtsmen and loftsmen and to define both the shape of the ship and its plating layout. Some of the half-models went back as far as the turn of the century and they ranged from destroyers, cruisers and battleships through to liners and Isle of Man boats.

These models had been in position for many years, but when one suddenly fell off the wall, narrowly missing Johnnie Black and an apprentice, Johnnie decided to get rid of them. When they were all taken down by the apprentices it was found that most of the securing screws were almost rusted away. Johnnie sent some of the half-models down to the gun mock-up shop for use in the making of scale model anchors etc. The others were sawn up for firewood. Upon reflection, this really was an act of historical vandalism but at the time no one though much about it.

I rescued one model, that of HMS Cassandra, a cruiser built in the yard in 1916 and secured it to a wall above my own bench. For a couple of years I stood my tea mug on this beautifully varnished half-model until one day the shipyard plant joiners arrived with orders to remove any models or half-models left in the loft. To this day I regret that I did not acquire some of the half-models before they were destroyed, and still wonder about the present whereabouts of the model of HMS Cassandra.

Gib Darragh came back to work for a few weeks but was taken ill again and died of a heart attack. With typical lack of forward planning the firm had left the department with no one suitable to take over as head foreman loftsman. Johnnie Black and other departmental foremen were all over sixty years old so the firm advertised the post, asking for an experienced person of between thirty-five and forty-five to apply. Only one or two men in the department came into this category, but they were not selected for an interview.

After a month or two had elapsed, Johnnie Black came round the shop floor accompanied by a tall, distinguished looking man whom he introduced as our new head foreman, Jim Foster. By a strange coincidence I had not only heard of Jim Foster but had even read about him in a book written by the famous yachtsman Uffa Fox. Mr Foster had been the head foreman loftsman at J Samuel White's shipyard where my fellow assistant carpenter on Orcades had served his apprenticeship. He had been involved in the loft work of the first all-welded yacht to be built in the world. This had been designed by Uffa Fox and built by White's for Mr Colman of Colman's Mustard during the 1930s, hence Mr Foster's mention in the book.

He came to Barrow about six months after White's yard had closed to take up a post in the new quality control department. No local men were given the chance to work in this new department, their skills were needed in their present jobs. Jim Foster was a quietly spoken Scotsman and was over sixty years old when he took over as head foreman loftsman. His first task in the new job was to refuse to enter the head foreman's office until it had been completely gutted, repainted and refurbished. This action was definitely a case of the new broom sweeping clean.

Jim Foster quickly established himself and we soon found out that he knew his loft work. Despite the fact he took over a long-established department which, it must be said, was hidebound with old-fashioned methods and traditions, he was well received by the workforce.

He was first ever head foreman to send a lorry load of timber back to the joiners shop. As I recall, the timber — light, thin, whitewood strips used for batten templates — was no better or worse than we usually received, but Jim Foster rejected the lot saying: "My men can only turn out a first-class job if they have first-class materials to work with." The next day and in future years the timber supplied to the mould loft was always of the highest quality and certainly helped us turn out a better, longer-lasting job than previously.

Gentleman Jim Foster had served his apprenticeship at the Ailsa Ship-building Company of Troon and when he arrived in Barrow he had about forty years supervisory experience behind him. He knew how to get things done and how to get the best out of his workforce.

Within twelve months of his arrival in the mould loft the whole building was renovated. The loft got a new insulated roof, which incorporated better natural lighting. There were new fluorescent lights installed, along with a new heating system, and the whole place was cleaned and painted. Plan desks and stools arrived for the workforce. Jim Foster acquired them from the ship drawing office, which at the time was having new equipment installed. In a short space of time our new head foreman had us working in good conditions and a happy atmosphere.

Shortly before Gentleman Jim's arrival, a grading system had been introduced whereby the loft department went on to three grades of pay instead of two. Jim Foster coped well with this new system, which at first was the cause of much discontent and argument when some of the loftsmen were dropped onto a lower grade. Every six months, when a grading review was due, he would upgrade two or three men. Within three years the loft department had a higher percentage of first and second grade men than any other department in the yard.

With my interest in yachts and boats, and having been shipmates with one of Jim's former apprentices, we got on well together and during our conversations on subjects of mutual interests I came to admire his communication skills and his philosophy.

"A quiet word can save a lot of trouble," Was one of his maxims. If you were in his office getting a chalk line or supply of pencils, he would say such things as: "I notice that some of the apprentices are leaving the shop early at lunchtime. Perhaps if someone had a word with them they could wait until I have left for my own lunch before they get a flyer (early start)." Sometimes his comment would be: "Some of the men are spending a lot of time smoking in the toilet area. Perhaps if there were only two or three men in the area together it might look better should a manager come into the loft." Such hints were always passed on and adopted.

These quiet words from Gentleman Jim were far better that a stand-up confrontation and certainly proved his other maxim: "Loyalty is like respect. You have to give it to earn it."

Jim Foster's laid-back methods of man management must have impressed the shipyard management because he was asked to stay on after his 65th birthday. Sadly, within a few months of this, he died suddenly while attending a head foreman's meeting in the yard. Many of the workforce attended the funeral of this likeable gentleman whose quiet methods of supervision and sensible interpretation of the rules made him many friends.

During the last twelve months of his reign as mould loft head foreman I had been loft shop steward and can state that I always had the utmost cooperation from Gentleman Jim, the man who gave and got respect.

When Johnnie Black retired at the age of sixty-five, workmen, foremen and managers from all over the yard came to pay their respects to a man who, as one manager put it: "Was a friend to all and the finest shipbuilder ever to work in the yard." Sadly, after only a few years retired, and still cheerful and unassuming during a long and painful illness, he died. Perhaps, as he looks down today from that great big shipyard in the sky, he despairs of what's happening in the yard now that computers have taken the place of loftsmen. Johnnie Black, shipbuilder extraodinaire, would probably smile and say: "Never mind, Barrow soccer are doing well." And so they should be, as the ashes of this remarkable man are scattered on Holker Street football ground.

There were many excellent tradesmen working in the loft during my time and probably veteran loftsman John Crossfield, of Walney, who, working until well past retirement age, could be classed as the best of the best. His last job was to lift the measurements and lines from the three pieces of the old Coniston steam yacht Gondola, then draw them on the loft floor for a complete new hull to be made in the West Shop.

I enjoyed my years working on the loft floor and could safely say that I worked on ships from the gestation period right through until the end of trials.

Chapter 11

Loftsman to Liner-off — Back to the Berths

THE title of liner-off means basically what it says: a man who lines off, or marks off, positions of structure or seatings for other tradesmen to work to. Most trades such as fitters, electricians, joiners, plumbers, sheetmetal workers and others had their own liner-offs, but the loftsman liner-off worked mainly on the ship structure servicing many other trades. Working from an office or cabin on the berths, his job encompassed such varied work as supplying information to the shipwrights and platers as they constructed the vessel and the marking of holes in the ship's hull for doors, access openings, sea inlets, and portholes. The line of the ship's waterline and the draughtmarks were also lined off by the loftsman liner-off.

Under construction at the time I went back on the berths was the cruise liner Copenhagen, the last merchant ship to be built in the yard. During her building time on the berth there had been several stoppages of work on her. This was not due, as you may surmise, to any fault of the workforce or unions but to the financial problems experienced by her Danish owners. She was launched without ceremony on 20 December, 1972. Mr Redshaw and the owners' representative were the only two people in the launch party. Copenhagen was part-fitted out at Barrow then taken to Newcastle for completion. Following her return she was laid up in Ramsden Dock for some months until her sale to the Russian Black Sea Company when she was renamed Odessa.

I recall getting the caulkers to cut off the steel letters of her original name, which were welded on her bow and stern. As the letters of her new name were in the Cyrillic alphabet I had to study the plan carefully to line off their positions. At the same time, as she lay at the old naval base berth in Ramsden Dock, I had to line off the position for the Russian hammer and sickle emblem on her funnel. This emblem was a prefabricated steel structure and was fitted by the shipwrights repair squad after being brought to the ship in the firm's Tug 9, skippered by shipwright Dennis Quayle. As the hammer and sickle was being fitted to the funnel of Odessa, and the new name was being welded on her bow and stern, the firm, for some reason, was vehement in its denial that the vessel had been sold to the Russians.

Over the next few years I worked as a liner-off on the destroyers Sheffield, Hercules and Cardiff in addition to several submarines. Hercules was a Type 42 class destroyer built for the Argentine Navy, but was more heavily armed than her sister vessels for the Royal Navy.

Working as a liner-off both on the berths and the dockside had its share of incidents. One job on HMS Sheffield was helping fellow liner-off Brian McGovern brighten up the lines of the ship's boot topping and waterline when the ship was on the floating dock. These lines, which define where the anti-fouling paint on the hull ceases and the grey paint of the topsides commences, had been referenced in by pop marks before her launch.

The red leaders and painters were applying the final coat of paint on Sheffield as we picked out the reference marks for them to work to. Despite our entreaties, pleas and suggestions, a couple of the red leaders would persist in painting over our new lines. Doing this job with a gang of painters above, below, ahead and behind us on a cold and windy winter's day did not really put us in a happy frame of mind. In addition, we were getting splashed and covered in grey paint and anti-fouling paint. When once again a red leader painted out the line we had so carefully put on, one of our labourers had had enough. He grabbed the red leader by the scruff of the neck and told him what would happen if he did it again. Tempers were, to say the least, getting rather frayed and it took the timely arrival of ship manager Derek Whalley to calm everyone down. For some time after this incident, relations between the painting department and the loft liner-offs were somewhat strained.

My last job on the Sheffield was again with Brian McGovern, lining off the identification number D80 on her hull. When Sheffield met her end during the Falklands conflict of 1982 there were many local workmen who regretted the loss of the destroyer they had fond memories of working on.

In 1975 I was transferred from the mould loft department back into the shipwrights department. This transfer was not entirely unexpected as relations between the head foreman loftsman and myself had never been of the best. As luck would have it I went from being a loftsman liner-off to a shipwright liner-off, working on HMS Invincible which was building at the top yard.

Shipwright liner-offs marked off and ordered material for the tradesmen of their own department, but they were only employed on surface craft, the loft department having the monopoly on submarines.

On Invincible I worked with and alongside many of my former shipwright mates. One such mate was The Count. He was always smartly dressed in sports coat and slacks, complete with white shirt and tie. When he arrived at work from his home town of Ulverston he used to change into overalls and working shoes. The works canteen was not for him.

At lunchtime he would remove his overalls and working shoes, polish his other shoes then, having carefully brushed himself down, would walk into town to dine at the Coop Cafe next to the Mail Office in Abbey Road. To describe The Count, words such as aristocratic, debonair, suave and sophisticated come to mind. You could imagine him playing the part of a stiff-upper-lip RAF officer and gentleman pilot who, having been captured by the enemy, makes a practice of tormenting his captors. His keen, incisive wit was often far above the heads of some of the over-zealous foremen for whom he worked.

After his lunch at the Coop Cafe his return to work would always be via the Derby Hotel or the Travellers Rest Hotel where he would consume two or three pints of best bitter to wash down his lunch. It was hard to define just how much work The Count got through, particularly on a Friday afternoon.

On Friday lunchtime he would always obtain a pass-out from work for 11.30am which gave him more time for dining and drinking. I once worked mates with him on Dreadnought and we got on well together, even though I usually came off the job twice as dirty as The Count, who could stay immaculately clean no matter what the job.

One story told about The Count was when he worked for Newall's Insulation Company in the yard during the early post-war period. With style, flair and aplomb, some five minutes or so before finishing time he would stroll confidently up the hill from Buccleuch Dock, nod politely and say goodnight to the works guard on the gate, and pass straight through. With his personality and panache, The Count was believed by the guard to be of managerial status and therefore was never questioned about his early leaving of the works. The early finishing came to an end one day when Archie Glenn, the Newall's manager, happened to be in the gatehouse when his employee passed through.

"Goodnight," said The Count to the guard.

"Where the hell are you going?" said Archie to The Count.

"Back to the ship," said The Count as he executed a 180 degree turn and strode smartly back down Devonshire Dock hill. You either liked, admired and appreciated The Count or you did not. I did, and found that beneath the surface lay a talented artist with a great sense of humour and a deep love of the countryside and environment.

In my family today is a lovely oil painting of a snow scene painted for me by The Count during a traumatic time in my life. The Count had many friends and when he died a few years before he was due to retire, the yard lost one of its more pleasant, helpful, colourful and — dare I say — flamboyant personalities. The Count was something of an enigma who had an unconventional approach to his work in the shipyard. Perhaps his epitaph could say that he was a man who did not suffer rules gladly.

I worked on Invincible from 1975, went down on her launch in 1977, then worked through to completion in 1980. With my laying-off of her lines in the mould loft and then the following years of her construction, fitting out and then trials, I realised that I had finally worked on a vessel from her gestation period right through until she was accepted by her owners.

Among the outfit shipwrights on Invincible was Lenny Mulholland, who originally came from the Belfast shipyard of Harland and Wolff. Lenny had the Irishman's dry sense of humour. An apprentice in the squad fitting out Invincible's magazines had, for weeks, been telling Lenny and his work-mates how he was to get his first motor cycle on his 18th birthday. Five minutes before starting time one warm July morning, the apprentice arrived in the shipwrights store looking every inch the part of a motor cycle rider straight from the TT Races. He was resplendent in a full-face helmet, black leather trousers, jacket and boots, and wearing a heavy scarf and gauntlets. Standing in the doorway he proudly and expectantly awaited comments. Lenny looked up from his *Daily Mirror*, eyed the lad from top to toe, then turning back to his paper in a half statement, half question said: "You came on the bus today then son?"

Following the completion of the Invincible I was transferred into the repair and docking squad where I worked with shipwright Mick Kitchen.

One job in this squad was the preparing of the floating dock for the docking of the submarines. Shortly after my arrival in this squad I came into work one morning to hear about an accident which had occurred on the submarine fitting out at the sub dock. With no serious accidents having taken place in the yard for some considerable time it came as a doubly unexpected shock to hear of a fatality. My friend and mate from previous years, John Rigg, had been tragically killed the previous evening when carrying out his duties as a safetyman shipwright. This tragedy brought many men back to the realisation that shipbuilding was still a hazardous occupation. Many of the yard's workforce attended John's funeral to pay their tribute to a likeable, hardworking personality whose good sense of humour made him the ideal workmate.

The shipwrights in the repair and docking squad handled and maintained the three work boats in the yard. Tug 9 and Tug 10 were purpose-built steel tugs and the other boat — named the Black Pig after the *Captain Pugwash* cartoon on TV by shipwright Frank Greenhalgh — was a 54ft-long ex-Admiralty harbour launch.

Tug 9 was skippered by shipwright Dennis Quayle who, apart from being one of the best all-round shipwrights in the yard, was arguably one of the finest boat handlers and seamen in the area. It was said that no matter what the weather or the load on tow, Dennis could bring his boat alongside a jetty so carefully and gently that he would not crack an egg.

My next move was back as an outfit shipwright at the top yard, under foreman shipwright Walter Cooper, on the first of class submarine HMS Trafalgar. I was aboard this vessel when she was launched on 1 July, 1981. A nasty accident could have occurred when the pilot, for some reason, omitted to authorise the release of the last drag chain wire. Tug 9 had passed the tow rope to the Liverpool tug, three of the four drag wires had been released, and Trafalgar was under way but with the last drag chain still holding her back. Shipwright John Croft was stationed at the slip and crouched down inside the superstructure awaiting the release order. Our desperate shouts to the pilot on top of the bridge fin appeared to be unheard as the strain on the drag chain slip increased.

Dennis Quayle spotted the danger and had a quick word with the pilot over the VHF radio on Tug 9. As soon as the pilot became aware of this potentially dangerous situation he ordered the release of the drag. This was easier said than done. The slip had been designed to operate with the weight pulling from forward but at this stage all the strain was on the side of the drag plate. John Croft finally managed to release the slip but not without a degree of difficulty and a certain amount of danger to himself. Tension on the heavy steel slips had been so great that the securing bolts had been stretched to the extent that they had to be burned out. The slip itself was so bent and distorted that it had to be scrapped. It was only due to the keen observation and quick thinking of Tug 9's skipper that no one was seriously hurt in this practically unnoticed situation.

Dennis Quayle worked on the yard's fleet of boats for twenty-two years until he took early retirement in 1984.

Towards the end of 1982 I left Trafalgar and was moved into the mock-up shop where full size sections of the submarines were constructed or mocked-up in wood. This mock-up work, originally solely a shipwrights work, had over the years been supplemented by the introduction of joiners.

In late 1982, only isolated areas of the submarines were built in the mock-up shop as gradually the work was being phased out and replaced by scale models built of plastic. To me the mock-up work was rather frustrating. Having worked on real submarines and having had to modify certain jobs to get them working, I could not really relate to making and fitting the unworkable jobs in timber.

After several months on this work I was approached by the head foreman loftsman and asked if I would consider going back in the department as a liner-off. By this time Jim Foster's successor had retired, and as the department appeared to be successfully managed, I accepted the offer. I must say that after nearly forty years in the yard this was the first time I had ever been asked if I would like to move to a new job.

MR LEN (later Sir Leonard) Redshaw, chairman of the firm, was once described as "a shipbuilder without equal and a man among men" (photo North West Evening Mail)

COUNCILLOR Bob Proudfoot, the Barrow boilermakers' union district delegate, was a skilled negotiator for his members (photo North West Evening Mail)

HERE Trafalgar takes to the water on 1 July 1981. The skipper of the firm's Tug 9 prevented what could have been a nasty accident by informing the pilot that he had not given the order to release the last drag chain (photo VSEL)

11 JULY 1988. During the largest ever strike at the yard the trade unions march to a mass meeting (photo North West Evening Mail)

Chapter 12

Them and Us — Management and Unions

NO ONE who worked in the Barrow shipyard could say that his or her life was never affected by the trade unions. Like them or hate them the unions, like the management, were an insuperable fact of shipyard life. On this basis one cannot write about shipyard life, shipyard ways and shipyard characters, without including the people who made up the often opposing forces of management and unions.

To start at the top Sir Leonard Redshaw has to stand out as the most significant personality ever to be at the helm of the Barrow shipyard. Probably like the Old Masters, his work was not appreciated until after his death, but from the 1940s until the late 1970s his influence was felt all over the yard.

The mid-60s signalled an era of change in the yard. Barrow had moved into the nuclear age with the building of Dreadnought. The yard was building the first of a new class of submarines, Valiant, when it announced in May 1963 that Barrow was to build the ballistic missiles submarines Repulse and Resolution.

Leonard Redshaw fought hard to obtain these orders and it is no under-statement to say that his efforts kept the yard in the lead in the field of submarine building. When these orders were placed the unions were as they had always been, fragmented and split but fighting as they always had for better pay and working conditions. Mr Redshaw, in the mid 60s, in an attempt to remedy this situation, called all the various trade union shop stewards together and proposed a package deal.

This was not a benevolent gesture on the part of the firm but a proposed productivity deal whereby the rates of pay for all trades would be evened out, apart from special allowances for certain jobs, marker-offs etc. Coinciding with the time of this proposed package deal the shipwrights union was going through the process of amalgamation with the boilermakers union.

Shortly before these proposals were mooted, the shipwrights had rejected their piecework system of work and had spent several weeks on a low time rate of pay. The amalgamation of the shipwrights and boilermakers brought to end the *esprit de corps* that existed within the trade union since its formation in the 1880s.

The older shipwrights of today will recall how apprentices were nurtured in the beliefs and customs of their union. Apprentices were always told that their trade was the second oldest profession and the most religious of all. Noah was a shipwright because he built the Ark and you can't go back in history further than that. Jesus was a carpenter, so that makes the trade a religious one. The quarterly meetings held in the Preston Street Club gave the shipwrights an opportunity to meet and discuss the problems relating specifically to their trade. Absentees from this meeting were fined 2/6d (12.5p) and the money collected went to their local benevolent fund.

Upon amalgamation, such meetings and union benefits such as sick pay and funeral benefit for wives were discarded and the comradeship of the trade was lost for ever. It should also be recorded that the trades affiliated to the shipwrights — ship riggers, sailmakers and ship drillers — were also amalgamated at the same time.

With amalgamation upon them the negotiations for the shipwrights at the package deal meeting were carried out by boilermakers district delegate Bob Proudfoot. Every union in the yard went along with this package deal, which could be discussed and amended annually. The rationalisation of pay rates meant that many men enjoyed a weekly pay increase of around £4.

This new deal was well received by the workforce and although some people had reservations it did bring a certain amount of stability into the yard, which meant that the Polaris submarine building programme was completed in record time.

The word strike is defined in my dictionary as to cease work in order to force a demand. For those involved in a strike it is an all-encompassing word. Over my working years in the yard I, like thousands of others, took part in many strikes, to use the word loosely. Everyone who has been involved in a strike will have different views and opinions about why they were not in work. Some will say they were locked out. Some will hold the view that the firm had created a situation, causing a walkout. Some will say they were laid off unfairly because of action taken by other trades, and some will say they were sent home for working to rule or for refusing to work overtime.

Space does not permit a detailed account of or even a list of the many strikes that occurred in the yard over the last fifty years. The full history of local trade unions has yet to be written and surely deserves to be while memories and records are still available.

Leaving the subject of strikes and returning to Sir Leonard Redshaw, the man who was once described as a big man in a big job. His dedication to the firm and his leadership qualities showed through in 1973.

In the late 60s the firm had set up Vickers Oceanics and was building and operating manned submarines of the Pisces class. In August 1973, Roger Chapman and Roger Mallinson were trapped on the sea bed, 1,575 feet down, after their submersible Pisces III was damaged during a recovery operation following a normal dive. For three and a half days, millions of people throughout the world followed the desperate attempts to rescue the two men trapped in the Atlantic Ocean, far deeper than any had previously survived on the sea bed. As soon as news of the accident reached Barrow, Sir Leonard, by then chairman of Vickers Shipbuilding, with Greg Mott the managing director of Vickers Oceanics, set up an operations room in an office in the director's corridor and began to organise the rescue operation.

Assisted by Tom Clark, the press officer for the company, the two men played an important part in the successful rescue of the two divers. Press conferences were held three times a day. Food and drinks were sent up to the operations room as trans-Atlantic telephone calls were made and accepted day and night. The respect and esteem in which Sir Leonard was held by navies, shipbuilders and governments throughout the world was displayed by the help he was offered in this dramatic salvage operation.

Men and equipment were rushed by air and sea from Britain, Canada, USA and Ireland. Two specially designed toggles for lifting the submersible were manufactures by platers in the yard and flown with all haste to the rescue ships standing by the stricken craft, far out in the Atlantic, 150 miles off Cork in Southern Ireland. Sir Leonard, Greg Mott and Tom Clark never left the premises or had any sleep until the word came through that the two men were safe.

Roger Chapman and Roger Mallinson had been trapped on the sea bed for seventy-six hours. For more than three days and nights the team in the operations room had pulled out all the stops and used all their knowledge and contacts to advise and assist in what was one of the most dramatic submarine rescues ever. At the conclusion of this successful operation, champagne was passed around to all involved including the typists, secretaries and telephone operators. In addition they received a letter of thanks from Sir Leonard.

The full story of this rescue is told in the book *No Time on our Side* by Roger Chapman.

Like him or hate him, you could not ignore Sir Leonard Redshaw. He once said to a meeting of all the shop stewards in the yard: "If the boilermakers would give me interchangeability within their union we can be the best yard in Europe. If I had full interchangeability within all the unions in the yard we could compete with any shipyard in the world." This did not happen during his reign but has been in operation since the privatisation of the yard.

Perhaps the words of Bob Proudfoot, boilermakers district delegate, could best sum up this outstanding man: "You may not like Redshaw but you

117

cannot deny that when it comes to shipbuilding he knows what he is talking about."

During the years I worked in the yard I found my working hours reduced from a 47-hour, five-and-a-half day week to a 37-hour, four-and-a-half day week. As an apprentice I had known unpaid bank holidays and one week's unpaid summer holiday. Over the years, each step forward in safety procedures, extra holidays with pay, free protective clothing, shorter working hours, paid time off for hospital appointments, family funerals and even house moving, had been gratefully received and appreciated. But all these benefits had to be negotiated and often fought for by the unions.

Without the hard work of dedicated trade unionists both locally and nationally few, if any, of these improvements to working life would have been implemented. Over the past few years the staff and workmen — them and us — have been brought closer together in many respects. Everyone has the same grade of toilet paper now!

Sir Leonard Redshaw will be remembered as being a dynamic leader of Barrow shipyard. He was once described as a man among men. The names of the many trade union officials and shop stewards who worked so hard to bring a better quality of life to their members, however, may never be recorded or remembered. But they, too, in their own way, helped the Barrow shipyard to become one that could, and did, compete with the best in the world.

— Chapter 13 —

Lay Offs and Pay Offs

"WE BUILD 'em, the other trades just decorate 'em," said the boilermakers in 1980, during an unsuccessful strike in support of a claim for a separate bonus system to the rest of the yard. It was not until I returned to the mould loft department as a liner-off in the new assembly shop, NAS, that I realised the true reason behind this statement.

In 1983 the NAS at the top yard was a place to avoid as much as possible. Unless it was raining or snowing heavily, or you had business inside the shop, you did not enter the NAS, you simply walked around it. The NAS was so called because of the refurbishment in the 1950s when it was altered from a platers shed into a shop for the building and assembly of large prefabricated ship units.

Although, over the years, the leaking roof was replaced, lighting improved, the floor concreted, new cranes installed and extensions added, little thought or effort had been put into tackling the problem of adequate ventilation. Consequently, when the shop was working at full capacity the scene inside could have been used as a setting for Dante's *Inferno*. On a windless day the smoke, fumes and heat from countless welders, gougers, grinders, burners and pre-heating coils, hung trapped under the roof like a cloud of low-lying mist shrouding a Lakeland fell. The noise in the NAS was entirely different from the noise of shipbuilding in the 1940s.

Basically, shipbuilding in those days was associated with the smell of sulphur from the riveting fires and the cacophony of the riveting and caulking hammers. Submarine construction in the 1980s has to be associated with the staccato stutter of the screwing up machine; the screaming shriek of high-speed carborundum grinders attacking high tensile steel; the spluttering, spattering, sibilant hiss of the arc-air gougers sending out a stream of red hot sparks and spewing out a cloud of toxic fumes. This then was the sound and smell of submarine building in the NAS.

All around the shop floor were various sections of submarines. Many were open-ended pressure hull sections lying flat on the floor and dotted, apparently haphazardly, around like giant slices of a Swiss roll cut off at varying thicknesses. Other sections were standing horizontally on wooden blocks and being pulled, jacked and shored into position ready for welding together to form an enormous steel pipe.

As you passed these sections you could feel the heat given off from the pre-heating coils, smell and taste the sickly gouging, grinding and welding fumes, and see the choking fog of smoke rising to join the all-pervading cloud hanging trapped under the roof. Perhaps this description of the NAS will help the reader to understand why, if at all possible, you walked around the New Assembly Shop.

Among this soul-subduing scene of submarine building were the men, mainly boilermakers and welders working with red-rimmed eyes hour after hour in temperatures ranging up to 160 degrees. These highly skilled top grade specialist welders such as Lol Slee and Joe Murphy, were once dubbed the Royal Family by Sir Leonard Redshaw. Reputedly, this title was given when he was asked: "Who are the men carrying little metal tubes (quivers or boxes) full of welding rods away from the welding rod store?"

"We call them the Royal Family," said Sir Leonard, "because they get more money than anyone else and think themselves a class above the other tradesmen."

Gougers such as Arthur Paxton in their hooded protective clothing and heavy gloves also worked in these extremely high temperatures on, and in, the sub units — and they had perhaps the dirtiest job of all. The firm did, however, install showers for their use and allowed them to finish work five minutes early to clean up. Other men in the units were hy-cycle grinders who cleaned up and polished the hardened tortured metal blasted away by their fellow tradesmen gougers.

Caulkers and burners such as Tony Coulter and Steve Spencely were among the men who could burn through a several inches thick steel pressure hull at any given angle to leave a finished cut within half a millimetre of a marked line. The other boilermakers, shipwrights, platers, drillers and liner-offs also worked in these conditions and their efforts in this extremely unpleasant environment certainly justified their "We build 'em" statement, when one made comparisons with, say, office workers who were given the same bonus payments.

Electricians also worked in the NAS. When they fitted the asbestos covered heating coils to the submarine units they wore hooded overalls, masks and gloves, apparently as protection against the dreaded poisonous asbestos. For some reason these precautionary measures were not deemed necessary for the other tradesmen who worked far closer to the heating coils as they gouged, burned, welded and monitored the units during assembly.

Mention of the people who worked in this environment must also include the cleaners who laboured at the never ending task of attempting to rid the shop of its perpetual coating of black carbon dust.

As I adapted — if one ever did — to the conditions in the NAS, I was able to renew my acquaintance with naval overseers such as Bill Biddles and John Norman, who checked and approved our measurements and marked lines before burning and welding authorisation was given. Their work was, to some extent, duplicated by staff members of the quality control department. Some of the older members of this department were pleasant experienced tradesmen with whom we could get along. After privatisation an increase in manpower of this and many other departments added something to the old adage which became modified to read: "A fool and a woman, and some quality control people, should not see a job half done."

At this period of my time in the yard I was still able to meet up with characters and personalities.

One personality was the plater nicknamed When I. He was so called because no matter what the conversation was he would interrupt by saying: "When I was working on . . ." or "When I was in the Navy . . ." etc. There was also old TST, or Hans (short for Hans Christian Anderson), who for many years enthralled his workmates, and indeed anyone who would listen, with his stories. "One Sunday morning when I was walking my dog in the sandhills at Roanhead, two wild geese flew overhead. Quick as a flash I whipped out my air pistol, specially adapted to be extra powerful, and firing from the hip the pellet passed through both birds killing them both. One fell straight down onto a rabbit, which it stunned, and the other bird fell into the sea and stunned a ten-pound salmon. My dog retrieved the first bird and the rabbit then swam out to sea and brought back the other bird and then the salmon, carrying them both in his mouth at once. Two geese, a rabbit and a ten-pound salmon with one shot."

Another story from TST was the time he helped bring a car to Barrow from Birmingham. The car was a Ford Prefect. Our hero tweaked the carburettor to tune it up properly then with his companion set off home. Several times on the way home he looked in the mirror and observed an E Type Jaguar following, but he always left it behind. When they arrived at Milnthorpe they stopped for fish and chips and had a pint in the Bull's Head. Coming out of the pub a man approached them and said: "Are you the driver of the Ford Prefect?" Getting an affirmative answer, the chap introduced himself as Stirling Moss, the champion racing driver, and said: "I'd like to shake your hand because I've never known anyone drive as fast and as well as you. I just couldn't catch you and I've followed you all the way from Birmingham."

One other story concerns his army service in Burma. He was leading a patrol of soldiers in the jungle to find out where the Japanese were camped. Silence was the order of the day because they dare not give their position away. Suddenly our hero and his men came face to face with a Bengal tiger, and they dare not shoot it in case the enemy were alerted. Quick as a flash the troop of soldiers turned around and ran for the safety of a small wooden hut and once inside slammed the door. The giant tiger leapt at the door with such force that its claws came straight through the woodwork. Our hero gave the tiger the *coup de grace* by clenching over the tiger's claws with the butt of his Tommy gun. Then, as the beast lay trapped against the door, he borrowed a bayonet from one of his men and stabbed it to death.

With stories like these it was no wonder that his character earned the nickname from a teller of fairy stories. His other nickname, TST, was also appropriate — Tall Story Ted.

In one department in the yard the foreman was "a bigger bore than the Mersey Tunnel and had the personality of a wet lettuce". This quote was from of his workmen. Each morning was the same. The foreman would come out of his office at 7.30am to go on his rounds. Always the same way round and, with only minor variations, always the same conversation. "Good morning," He would say, "It's wet-dry-hot-cold-windy outside." The only variation applied to the weather. "You're getting on OK?" Without a pause for an answer he would then say: "If you want anything see Ken." Ken was the chargehand and liner-off. Then moving on the same conversation would be enacted at the next workbench and varied but little during his afternoon rounds.

One workman who was not really happy in this department — there was more overtime outside on the berths — persuaded the departmental painter to paint a sign to go above his bench. The sign, in bold lettering, read Hebrews XIII v 8. Every time the foreman did his rounds, conversing in the same unexciting manner, the tradesman would put his hands together in an attitude of piety then roll his eyes towards heaven and the sign above his bench. If the foreman, a staunch churchgoer and freemason, ever noticed the sign or even understood it he never let on. The pattern of life for him and the workman continued until the foreman retired.

Today the department, like many others in the yard, has ceased to exist. However, this story could be used as an example that at least one workman in the yard knew his bible, even if his beliefs were not always used in the right context. Hebrews XIII v 8 Jesus Christ. The same yesterday, the same today and the same forever more.

There are many more stories associated with the shipyard men and shipyard life, but perhaps the one of shipwright Paddy Maguire, a man who could say anything to anybody and get away with it, best illustrates the humour of the Barrow workmen.

One of the labourers, who had been off work for a few days, came into work on the Thursday lunchtime to collect his wages. When asked by Paddy the reason for his absence he replied: "My wife has just died." Paddy, who knew of his unhappy marriage, said: "Well you want to put some money on the horses while your luck's in."

Between the years 1986, when the yard was privatised, and 1988, when the yard's largest ever strike took place, it was said that if you could think of a name for a department you could start one.

I recall one instance where three staff members from different departments came in on overtime one morning to check out plates being unloaded from a lorry. This work had previously always been done by the plater and his helper. It is also on record that three departments were formed to take over the work of the labourer, or handyman, who would normally collect finished jobs from around the yard at the request of his foreman or liner-off and bring them to the store on the departmental lorry.

In the latter part of the 1980s the North-West Evening Mail headlines boasted of Boomtown Barrow as workers were recruited from Tyneside and the Clyde. Most of them were lured to the town with promises of work until the 21st century. As this boom continued, management, with apparently no understanding of the local community, began to attempt to force through many ideas and work practices that were totally unacceptable to the workforce.

The company announced its intention to replace flexible holidays, which the workforce had enjoyed since 1983, with a return to the old system of a fixed holiday. This ultimatum by the privatised company was seen by the trade unions as a first attempt to operate new working practices and a move to stamp its authority on the workforce and the unions once and for all.

Battle lines were drawn and the result was a three-month strike in the summer of 1988. This was the first strike in the firm's history to involve all unions, including blue and white collar workers. In the end a return to fixed holidays was accepted, although a phased introduction was conceded with some extra days leave.

Many stories are told of the strike, which will remain in the memories of local men for many years to come. In the book *The Strike*, published by the Barrow Trade Unions, Roger Henshaw, the regional officer MSF and chairman No 31 District Committee Confederation of Shipbuilding and Engineering Unions, says: "This was a strike led by a rank and file who saw the fixed holiday issue as the final insult following years of provocation from an employer who, at that time, favoured imposition rather than negotiation."

The 13,000 trade unionists who were involved all have their own versions of what was the cause and what was achieved by the firm or the unions.

The welders, about 400 in all, had been on unofficial strike a few days before the main strike began on 8 June and continued their stoppage for several weeks after the major strike had ceased on 30 August. Their claim was for extra heat allowances.

One fact at least emerged from this dramatic strike which affected so many workers whose livelihood was dependent on the yard. In 1986, 82 per cent of the workforce had purchased shares, but by the time of the company's annual general meeting in December 1988, the proportion of worker shareholders was down to 23 per cent.

After the strike, recruitment of labour continued but the writing was on the wall when in 1989 news of the removal of the Berlin Wall came through. As the cold war receded and defence spending came under review, the future of VSEL began to look uncertain. The local trade unions, who had commissioned a study of possible alternative work for the yard, had their work derided by Dr Rodney Leach. Dr Leach suffered a heart attack during the strike and he later left the yard making way for Noel Davies to take over as chief executive.

It was during the strike that the humour of the local shipbuilders came through, despite the hardships suffered by men and their families. Roger Henshaw, chair of the local Confed, said to a mass meeting of strikers held at Cavendish Park: "You can always tell the people who are on strike. They're all sunburned and covered in paint."

The same mass meeting passed a most unusual resolution which received unanimous support: "This management has just got up our noses and the sooner they get a plane, train, boat or car out of Barrow the better". The company's logo, VSEL, was said to mean Very Soon Emslie's Leaving. Emslie was the yard's industrial relations director. Eventually he did leave.

Despite the feelings of the workforce with regard to management at the time of the strike, it should be noted the Mr Jim Glasgow, Dr Leach's deputy, was a highly respected Barrovian and his presence in negotiations was approved by all the Confed members and shop stewards.

In the early months of 1990 the workforce had grown to a peak of 14,300 and the Trident submarine programme was in full production. The ending of the cold war meant that the writing was not only on the wall but that the message was getting through that the firm would either have to find new work quickly, by diversifying, or there would have to be a reduction in the workforce. The trade unions took no comfort in the fact that they had been proved correct with their alternative work study of 1988.

In 1991 came the announcement that some 5,000 job losses could be expected in the next three years as the Trident submarine building programme ran down. The North-West Evening Mail then carried the headline Blues Over Barrow.

All those workmen on procedure, and many who were not, were called up in front of their managers and given a brown envelope containing their redundancy notice and told they had one-and-a-half hours to get their gear together and leave the yard. The old time workmen during the depression years of the 30s used to tell of how they were allowed two hours to collect and sharpen their tools after being given notice.

The world had changed.

Passenger liners like steam engines were things of the past, gone for ever and only to be remembered by a fast disappearing generation, or to be preserved in museums or in model form.

Since the redundancies began in 1991, and up to the summer of 1995, around 9,000 jobs have been lost at VSEL. Yet some of those directly affected still kept a sense of humour — albeit black.

In my own case I was lucky enough to be in a position to take voluntary redundancy.

Over a period of forty-four years in the yard I had worked with, and for, the best of the best and had come into contact with only a few people who could be classed as the worst of the worst. I had worked on many ships, known many people, seen many once old and established trades disappear and had witnessed the introduction of many new working practices. For my efforts during those years the firm had given me a trade which enabled me to see the world on the passenger liners I had helped to build. I had been in work for forty-four years and had always been paid for that work. I had been given a tea mug and an inscribed gold watch, which I had to ask for because the firm had lost my records. And three months after my departure I was given a long service certificate, illegibly signed by someone I had never met.

One wet summer afternoon, just as I was enjoying my afternoon brew and watching an old black and white film on TV, there was a knock at the door. A VSEL employee, with a job title that sounded something like deputy assistant personnel operations retirement counselling manager, was walking the streets knocking at many doors handing out long service certificates much like a Jehovah's Witness passing out bible tracts. I thanked him for mine and went back to my film.

Perhaps in this book I have been able to capture and record just something of life in the Barrow shipyard as seen through the eyes of an ordinary workman on the shop floor. Although the accent has been mainly on the shipbuilding side of the yard I am sure that many of those who worked in the engineering part will be able to relate to and recall some of the people and events which occurred during the past fifty years.

If I have offended anyone I apologise.

In any person's working lifetime there are periods of humour, tragedy, despondency, sadness, humiliation, frustration and despair. Yet remaining in tandem with these emotions are memories and the satisfaction of a job well done, coupled with the hope that there will be work for the others who follow on behind.

Since I first started in Barrow shipyard in 1944 there have been many changes in the world and many changes in shipbuilding practices.

Even as this book was being prepared for publication, news came through that VSEL had been taken over by GEC. The consequences for the yard and the town have yet to materialise.

It is my fervent hope that in fifty years time another person will write of his experiences in the Barrow shipyard and be able to say: "The man still wants his boat."